J. T. Sunderland
Hyde Park Ills
Dec 26" 1865.

THE

HOLY AND PROFANE STATES.

BY

THOMAS FULLER.

WITH

SOME ACCOUNT OF THE AUTHOR
AND HIS WRITINGS.

BOSTON:
LITTLE, BROWN AND COMPANY.
1864.

CAMBRIDGE:
STEREOTYPED BY H. O. HOUGHTON.

Presswork by John Wilson & Son, Boston.

ADVERTISEMENT.

IN order to bring this volume within a reasonable compass, portions, including the Lives, have been omitted, as less peculiar and interesting. Many passages and a few chapters have been excluded, as incompatible with the refined delicacy of modern manners. The most valuable parts, however, it is believed, are retained, everything, indeed, which readers in general, at the present day, would wish to have inserted.

To ascertain the true text, the editions of 1642 and 1648 have been carefully collated.

CONTENTS.

SOME ACCOUNT

OF THE

LIFE AND WRITINGS

OF

THOMAS FULLER.

THOMAS FULLER, the author of the following work, was an eminent historian and divine of the Church of England, in the stormy times of Charles I. and the Commonwealth. He was born in 1608, at Aldwinkle, in Northamptonshire, a town which a few years later acquired the additional celebrity of being the birthplace of Dryden. After being initiated in the rudiments of learning by his father, who was the minister of the parish, he was sent, at the early age of twelve years, to Queen's College, Cambridge, where he applied himself to his academic exercises with extraordinary diligence and success. Soon after he had taken the degree of Master of Arts, in 1628, he was chosen minister of St. Bennet's parish, in the town of Cambridge; "and here," says the author of his Life published in 1661, "by the most sublime divinity, in the most ravishing elegancies, he attracted the audience of the University, and became a very popular preacher at those years when others are scarce publicly known." In 1631, he made his first appearance as an author, in a poem entitled "David's hainous Sin, heartie Repentance and heavie Punishment," (thin 8vo). Soon afterwards he left Cambridge, on being presented to the rectory of Broad-Windsor, in Dorsetshire, where he discharged his ministerial duties for several years with great fidelity and acceptance. In 1640, appeared his "Historie of the Holy Warre," (folio,) which met with a favorable reception, and passed through three editions in a few years.

He was now induced, by the ferment in the nation, which indicated an approaching civil war, to remove to London, where he expected to enjoy greater security than in his country residence, and at the same time might have more ready access to the works and conversation of the learned; those "standing and walking libraries," as he quaintly calls them. In the metropolis he soon acquired great reputation as a preacher, and was chosen lecturer of the Savoy, in the Strand. "Here," says the author of his Life, "he gave such general satisfaction, became so famous, and was thronged with such distant congregations, that those of his own cure were in a manner excommunicated from their own church, unless their timeous diligence kept pace with their devotions; the Doctor affording them no more time for their extraordinaries on the Lord's day than what he allowed his habitual abstinence on all the rest. He had in his narrow chapel two audiences, one without the pale, and another within; the windows of that little church and the sextonry so crowded, as if bees had swarmed to his mellifluous discourse."

Fuller was a member of the Convocation that assembled in 1640, to make new canons for the better government of the church, and was one of the select committee; but disapproved of some of the steps taken by the Convocation. This, however, did not arise from a want of zeal in his attachment to the King's cause. Of this he gave abundant evidence by his exertions, in public as well as in private, to serve the royal interests. With this view, after the King had left London with a determination to commence hostilities against the Parliament, Fuller, on the anniversary of his Majesty's inauguration, preached a sermon at Westminster Abbey from 2 Sam. xix. 30: "Yea, let them take all, so that my Lord the King return in peace." This sermon, which was printed, gave great offence to the Parliament party, and brought the preacher into some danger. About this time, 1642, he published his "Holy State," (folio,) which passed rapidly through four editions. In the year 1643, after finding that, to prevent being silenced and ejected, as other royalists had been, he must take an oath against which his conscience protested, he withdrew to the King at Oxford, by whom he was well received. His Majesty having been apprised of his abilities as a preacher, expressed a desire to hear him, and Fuller accordingly preached before him at St. Mary's Church. On this occasion he incurred the censure of the royalists, for being, as they conceived, too lukewarm in their cause; whilst in London, as we have seen, he exposed himself to the resentment of the opposite party by his zeal for the King's service. It has hence been fairly concluded that he was an advocate for measures of conciliation, which did not accord with the views of either party. His own remark, on another occasion, may be applicable to this: "He is generally accounted an impartial arbitrator who displeases both sides." But when he found that there were no hopes remaining of any accommodation, he resolved to recover the opinion of his steady attachment to the royal cause by following the fortunes of the King's army. He accordingly obtained a letter of recommendation to Sir Ralph Hopton, who appointed him his chaplain.

Whilst discharging the duties of this office, he omitted no opportunity that offered of pursuing his studies and gathering materials for his historical works. "Whilst he was in progress with the King's army," says his biographer, "his business and study there was a kind of errantry; having proposed to himself a more exact collection of the Worthies of England, in which others had waded before, but he resolved to go through. In what place soever therefore he came, of remark especially, he spent most of his time in views and researches of their antiquities and church monuments; insinuating himself into the acquaintance, which frequently ended in a lasting friendship, of the learnedest and gravest persons residing within the place, thereby to inform himself fully of those things he thought worthy the commendation of his labors. It is an incredible thing to think what a numerous correspondence the Doctor maintained and enjoyed by this means. Nor did the good Doctor ever refuse to light his candle, in investigating truth, from the meanest person's discovery. He would endure contentedly an hour's or more impertinence from any aged church-officer, or other superannuated people, for the gleaning of two lines to his purpose. And though his spirit was quick and nimble, and all the faculties of his mind ready and answerable to that activity of dispatch, yet in these inquests he would stay and attend those circular rambles till they came to a point; so resolute was he bent to the sifting out of abstruse antiquity. Nor did he ever dismiss such adjutators or helpers, as he pleased to style them, without giving them money and cheerful thanks besides."

After the loss of the battle on Cheriton Down, in 1644, his general, now Lord Hopton, drew the remains of his army to Basing House, the seat of the Marquis of Worcester, where he left his chaplain; who animated the garrison to so vigorous a defence of that place when it was soon afterwards besieged by Sir William Waller, that the latter was obliged to abandon his enterprise, with the loss of more than a thousand men. When afterwards the King's army was driven into Cornwall, Fuller had leave to retire to Exeter, where he resumed his studies, and preached constantly with great satisfaction to the citizens. Whilst he resided at Exeter, his company and conversation were much courted by persons of all ranks, and indeed, wherever he was, the cheerfulness and facetiousness of his temper, added to his wit and learning, made him generally beloved. In short, he was so engaging and had such a fruitful faculty of begetting wit in others, when he exerted it himself, that he made his associates pleased with their own conversation as well as his; his blaze kindled sparks in them, till they admired at their own brightness; and when any melancholy hours were to be filled up with merriment, it was said, in the vein he could sometimes descend to, that the Doctor made every one *Fuller*. In 1645, he published at Exeter his "Good Thoughts in Bad Times." *

When Exeter was obliged to surrender to the Parliament forces under Sir Thomas Fairfax, in 1646, Fuller was permitted, without any loss or interruption, to remove to London. Here he met with a cold reception from his former parishioners at the Savoy, probably on account of the part which he had taken in politics; and found his lectureship filled by another person. In 1650, he published "A Pisgah-Sight of Palestine, and the Confines thereof, with the History of the Old and New Testament, acted thereon," (folio); in 1651, "Abel Redivivus, or the Dead yet Speaking: the Lives and Deaths of the modern Divines," (4to); and in 1656, "The Church History of Britain from the Birth of Jesus Christ until the Year 1648"; to which were subjoined, "The History of the University of Cambridge since the Conquest,"

* In 1647, appeared his "Good Thoughts in Worse Times," and at the Restoration in 1660, "Mixt Contemplations in Better Times." These three pieces were republished in a small volume by William Pickering, London, 1830.

and "The History of Waltham Abbey in Essex, founded by King Harold," (folio). Bishop Nicolson, in his "English Historical Library," observes of Fuller's "Church History": "Through the whole he is so full of his own wit, that he does not seem to have minded what he was about. If a pretty story comes in his way that affords scope for clinch and droll, off it goes with all the gayety of the stage, without staying to inquire whether it have any foundation in truth or not; and even the most serious and most authentic parts of it are so interlaced with pun and quibble, that it looks as if the man had designed to ridicule the annals of our Church into fable and romance. Yet if it were possible to refine it well, the work would be of good use, since there are in it some things of moment hardly to be had elsewhere." *

In 1660, Fuller accompanied his patron, Lord Berkley, to the Hague, to congratulate Charles II. on his restoration to the throne. Soon afterwards he was appointed chaplain to the King, created Doctor of Divinity at Cambridge, by mandamus, and destined to the Episcopal bench. This last preferment, however, was prevented by his death, which took place August 16, 1661, in the fifty-fourth year of his age. The year after his death was published his principal literary work, "The History of the Worthies of England," (folio,) † a work valuable

* An elaborate vindication of Fuller from Nicolson's and Heylin's attacks on his writings may be seen in the *Biographia Britannica*.

† A new edition of "The Worthies" was published in London, 1811, in two volumes quarto, with a few explanatory notes, by John Nichols.

alike for the solid information it affords relative to the provincial history of the country, and for the profusion of biographical anecdote of men and manners; though Bishop Nicolson says, that "the lives of his greatest heroes are commonly misshapen scraps, mixed with tattle and lies."*

Dr. Fuller's person was tall and well-made; his presence stately and majestic; and his manner frank and unaffectedly polite. His disposition was amiable and benevolent, and his conduct highly commendable in his domestic and social relations. We have already noticed the esteem in which he was held as an instructive and entertaining companion. His learning and ingenuity were considerable, his imagination lively, and his memory remarkably retentive. "He was a walking library," says his biographer, "but sometimes required turning over to attain the contents."

Of the strength of Fuller's memory such marvellous stories are recorded as almost stagger credibility. It is said that he could repeat five hundred strange and unconnected words, after twice hearing them; and could preach a sermon verbatim, which he had heard only once. In passing to and fro, from Temple Bar to the farthest end of Cheapside, he once undertook to mention all the signs over the shops, as they stood in order, on both sides of the way, repeating them either backwards or forwards; and performed his task with perfect exactness. In the Diary of Samuel Pepys, Esq., recently published, the writer says: "Jan. 22, 1661. I met with Dr.

* See note on page 13.

Thomas Fuller. He tells me of his last and great book that is coming out: that is, the History of all the Families in England; and could tell me more of my own than I knew myself. And also to what perfection he hath now brought the art of memory; that he did lately to four eminently great scholars dictate together in Latin upon different subjects of their proposing, faster than they were able to write, till they were tired; and that the best way of beginning a sentence, if a man should be out, and forget his last sentence, (which he never was,) that then his last refuge is to begin with an *Utcunque.*"

The Doctor making a visit to the committee of sequestrators sitting at Waltham, in Essex, they soon fell into a discourse and commendation of his great memory; to which he replied, "'Tis true, gentlemen, that fame has given me the report of a memorist, and, if you please, I will give you an experiment of it." They all accepted the motion, and told him they should look upon it as an obligation, praying him to begin. "Gentlemen," says he, "I will give you an instance of my memory in the particular business in which you are employed. Your worships have thought fit to sequester an honest but poor cavalier parson, my neighbor, from his living, and committed him to prison. He has a large family of children, and his circumstances are but indifferent. If you will please to release him out of prison, and restore him to his living, I will never forget the kindness while I live." *

"But what was most strange and rare in him,"

* Basil Montagu's *Selections*, p. 316.

says his biographer, "was his way of writing, which was somewhat like the Chinese, from the top to the bottom of the page. The manner thus: he would write next the margin the first word of every line, down to the foot of the paper; then beginning at the head again, would so perfectly fill up every one of the lines, as, without spaces, interlineations, or contractions, but with the full and equal length, would so aptly connect and conjoin the ends and beginnings, that the sense would appear as complete and as much to his mind, he would say, as if he had writ it after the ordinary manner, in a continued series." *

The following delineation of Fuller's character as a writer is extracted from the "Retrospective Review," Vol. III. p. 50:—

"If ever there was an amusing writer in this world, the facetious Thomas Fuller was one. There was in him a combination of those qualities which minister to our entertainment, such as few have ever possessed in an equal degree. He was, first of all, a man of extensive and multifarious reading; of great and digested knowledge, which an extraordinary retentiveness of memory preserved ever ready for use, and considerable accuracy of judgment enabled him successfully to apply. He was also, if we may use the term, a very great anecdote-monger; an indefatigable collector of the traditionary stories related of eminent characters, to gather which, his biographers inform us, he would listen contentedly for

* Burnett's *Specimens of the Old English Prose Writers*, Vol III. p. 172; and *Biographia Britannica.*

hours to the garrulity of the aged country-people whom he encountered in his progresses with the King's army. With such plenitude and diversity of information, he had an inexhaustible fund for the purposes of illustration, and this he knew well how to turn to the best advantage. Unlike his tasteless contemporaries, he did not bring forth or display his erudition on unnecessary occasions, or pile extract on extract, and cento on cento, with industry as misapplied as it was disgusting. With Fuller, a quotation always tells: learning with him was considered as a sort of mortar to strengthen, interlace, and support his own intellectual speculations, to fill up the interstices of argument, and conjoin and knit together the corresponding masses of thought; not as a sort of plaster to be superinduced over the original products of his mind, till their character and peculiarities were lost amid the integuments which enveloped them. So well does he vary his treasures of memory and observation, so judiciously does he interweave his anecdotes, quotations, and remarks, that it is impossible to conceive a more delightful checker-work of acute thought and apposite illustration, of original and extracted sentiment, than is presented in his works. As a story-teller, he was most consummately felicitous. The relation which we have seen for the hundredth time, when introduced in his productions, assumes all the freshness of novelty, and comes out of his hands instinct with fresh life, and glowing with vitality and spirit. The stalest jest, the most hackneyed circumstance, the repetition of which by another would only provoke our nausea, when adopted by him, receives a redintegration of essence not less miraculous than the conversion of dry bones into living beings. Wherever we dip in his works, we are certain to meet with some narrated incident or apothegm to detain us, and we are insensibly led on from anecdote to anecdote, and from witticism to witticism, without the power to put the book upon the shelf again. How delightful must have been the conversation of Fuller, varied as it was with exuberance of knowledge, enlivened with gossiping, chastened by good sense, and sparkling with epigrammatical sharpness of wit, decorated with all its native fantastical embroidery of humorous quaintness. We verily declare for ourselves, that, if we had the power of resuscitating an individual from the dead to enjoy the pleasure of his conversation, we do not know any one on whom our choice would sooner fall than Fuller.

"Of human life and manners, through all their varieties, he was also a most sagacious and acute observer; and the quantity of vigorous and just observation, in this department of inquiry alone, contained in his works, it is hardly possible to calculate with correctness or appreciate with justice. He united the cool penetration of the philosophical speculatist with the less erring because less refined contemplation of the practical experimentalist in the ways of man. He was learned, yet his learning did not take away his perspicuity in judging of the modes of every-day existence; he was indefatigable in literature, yet amidst his pursuits he found leisure to look into life with the acuteness of a Rochefoucault; he was addicted to meditation, yet he never was blinded to the observation of things without while occupied with the abstractions within. More profundity of remark, more accuracy of discernment, more justness of perception, than this topic always produces from his pen, it would be difficult elsewhere to find. Few scholars excelled more in sound and practical good sense, and consequently very few ever coined maxims of more irresistible and incontrovertible wisdom. To him the whole complete machinery, which composes the great work of existence, in all its parts, springs, and dependencies, lay exposed, and no subtlety in its regulations could deceive his intuitive quickness, no artificial intermingling of its interest could obscure his unerring penetration.

"But great as all these his endowments were, his qualifications of authorship, it is not perhaps to any of them that our chief satisfaction in reading the works of Fuller can justly be attributed. Others, many others, have doubtless possessed them in an equal if not in a superior degree, and the attractions of our author carry a peculiar individuality about them which no other can share or divide with him. These particular attractions which he alone monopolized, are doubtless the results of his unrivalled facetiousness and quaintness. The praises of wisdom and learning he must ever divide with countless multitudes, and in the pages of multitudes of writers may equal proofs of that learning and wisdom be met with. But for the facetiousness which breaks forth on all themes and subjects, and which hides itself but to burst forth again, like the river Arethusa, in all the creamy effervescence of sparkling frothiness, — which throws over his gravest disquisitions an air of irresistible jocularity, and over his most solemn adjurations an appearance of lurking and irrepressible slyness, — which diffuses over the obscure duskiness of church history a quaint oiliness of conceit, and enriches even geographical barrenness by its everlasting fecundity of wit; — for the hearty and chuckling fulness of mirth which catches at a joke as a boy does at a butterfly, and impresses every possible play of words of necessity into its service; — for the sedulous and resolute quest after humor which no consideration could divert or stop, and which would at any time spoil a good argument, or burlesque a serious observation, to hitch in an epigram, good, bad, or indifferent, — where shall we search but in the pages of the inimitable, the incomparable Fuller? It is not because he is generally successful in his attempts to be witty that we experience this gratification and delight, for nine of his attempts out of ten are certain to be complete failures; nor can it arise from the trueness of his wit, for commonly it consists of little more than puns, quibbles, and antitheses: it is not certainly from these, but from other causes that our satisfaction originates, from his glorious and enthusiastic intrepidity in his sallies to the land of humor, from his bold and determined Quixotism after wit and facetiousness, from his readiness to grasp at anything which bore the most distant resemblance to them, from his buoyant and eternal spirit of drollery, from his indefatigable and adventurous knight-errantry which would traverse the whole universe for wit, from his peculiar singleness of observation, which could see

'Humor in stones, and puns in everything.'

"He absolutely communicates something of his own fervor to his reader: it is almost impossible to read his works without going along with him in his hunt for jokes, and without participating in his satisfaction when he has found them. His quaint facetiousness was communicable to everything. Graft it on whatever tree he chose, and it would bud out, blossom forth, and luxuriate. Like a fisherman, he threw out his capacious net into the ocean of wit, and rejected nothing that it brought up, however miscellaneous or motley were its contents; pleased, and perhaps thinking that others would be pleased, with their variety. There is, besides, such an apparent self-satisfaction discernible throughout his works — we can almost fancy we see him chuckling over his forthcoming jests as they successively issue from his brain, preparing us by his triumphant exultation for the stroke which is to follow; or revelling in uncontrolled and uncontrollable merriment over the vagaries of which he had discharged his head by communicating them to paper. Such was the disposition of Fuller. The qualities of mind which would in another have produced a buffoon, in him, without losing their power of entertainment, lost all their grosser and more offensive traits, and became, from their very superfetation, less imbued with the rankness of farce. To him the language of jocularity had something of the gravity of earnest: it was his own vernacular idiom, in which everything which issued from his mind was clothed; it was something so intimately connected with him, that all attempts to strip it off would be useless; something settled and fixed in his intellect, and stamping and marking its whole character. By being therefore more generalized, it had less of marked purport and design, and as it was assumed on all subjects was indecorous on none. Fuller, we think, would hardly have scrupled to crack a joke upon the four Evangelists; but certain we are, it would have been without any idea of indecency or intention of irreverence.

"This characteristic peculiarity is equally visible in all his productions, from his 'Holy War' to his 'Worthies,' and consequently they are all almost equally entertaining. His 'Holy War' and 'Church History,' particularly the last, are two of the most agreeable works we know; replete, besides their Fullerism, with perspicacious observation, profound thought, deep discernment, and narrative power. There are specimens of historical painting in these works which perhaps have never been excelled, conceived with great energy and executed with happiness. In his delineation of characters, he exhibits such unrivalled acumen, ability, and penetration, together with such candor and uprightness of judgment, that it is difficult which most to admire, his sagacity or his sincerity. His 'Pisgah-Sight of Palestine,' which is also in part an historical work, is a happy elucidation of what Fuller always excelled in, sacred story: and no work of his better displays the riches of his mind or the plenitude and fertility of its images. His 'Worthies' is, we believe, more generally perused than any of his productions, and is perhaps the most agreeable; suffice to say of it, that it is a most fascinating storehouse of gossiping, anecdote, and quaintness; a most delightful medley of interchanged amusement, presenting entertainment as varied as it is inexhaustible. His 'Good Thoughts in Bad Times,' and lesser works, are all equally excellent in their way, full of admirable maxims and reflections, agreeable stories, and ingenious moralizations.

"It was, however, in biography that Fuller most excelled. If he was frequently too careless and inaccurate in his facts, it was not from heedlessness as to truth, which no one reverenced more than he did, but because he considered them but as the rind and outward covering of the more important and more delicious stores of thinking and consideration which they inwardly contained; because he thought life too short to be frittered away in fixing dates and examining registers: what he sought was matter convertible to use, to the great work of the improvement of the human mind, not those more minute and jejune creatures of authenticity, which fools toil in seeking after, and madmen die in elucidating. In this he has been followed by a great biographical writer of the last age, with whom he had more points than one in common. Leaving therefore such minor parts of biography for the investigation of others, and seizing only on the principal events, and those distinguishing incidents or anecdotes which mark a character in a moment, and which no one knew better than Fuller to pick out and select, he detailed them with such perspicuity and precision, and commented upon them with such accuracy of discrimination, strength of argument, and force of reason, and threw around them such a luminous and lambent halo of sparkling quaintness, shining upon and playing about the matter of his thoughts, and inspirited them with such omnipresent jocularity and humor, that, of all the biographical writers of his age, he is, in our opinion, infinitely the best. After the perusal of the more polished, but certainly not more agreeable biographers of modern times, we always recur with renewed gusto and avidity to the Lives of our excellent author, as to a feast more substantial, without being less delicious.

"The work which we have selected as the subject of this review is as well calculated to evince the justice of the foregoing remarks as any of his lucubrations. Perhaps, upon the whole, it is the best of his works; and certainly displays, to better advantage than any, his original and vigorous powers of thinking. It consists of two parts — the 'Holy and the Profane State': the former proposing examples for imitation; and the latter their opposites, for our abhorrence. Each contains characters of individuals in every department of life, as 'the father,' 'husband,' 'soldier,' and 'divine'; lives of eminent persons, as illustrative of these characters; and general essays. In his conception of character he has followed Bishop Earle and Sir Thomas Overbury, but his manner of writing is essentially different. This species of composition was very near akin to what has been called the school of metaphysical poetry, sprung up into existence about the same time, and went out of fashion along with it. It was composed of the same materials, and regulated by nearly the same principles. Did our limits allow us, we do not know a more interesting and yet undeveloped subject for speculation than the concurrent and dependent styles of prose and poetry which prevailed from the accession of James I. till after the Restoration, and which were in truth all referable to one original. At present we can only observe that the care of the writers of characters was to crowd together the most motley assemblage of ideas in the smallest possible space; to concentrate, in one series of links, the most multitudinous spangles of conceit; to pour forth all the subject presented in one close intertexture of ideas, which received at once point from their wit, and smartness from their brevity. By these means the thoughts are often so much compressed as to produce obscurity, or at least are defrauded of their due quantum of verbal clothing. Their very multitude produces confusion, and we are prevented from taking notice of each particularly by their cluster and conglomeration, and by the rapidity with which they alternately approach and recede. Thought succeeds thought; the most recondite metaphors are squeezed into an epithet or an adjective; one point is elbowed out by another, 'like pricks upon the fretful porcupine,' till in mental dizziness and distraction we are obliged to bring our perusal of the book to an end.

Of this method of writing, Butler's "Hudibras" is an enlarged specimen, — that ever-standing monument of the lavish prodigality of wit.

"It may at first appear rather surprising that Fuller, fond as he was of pointed quaintness, and with such exuberance of images as he was possessed of, should have deserted this popular style of character-writing, and introduced in the stead of its curt and contracted sharpness his own more easy, but less ambitious, diffuseness. But this, we think, may easily be accounted for. His intellectual plenitude was too great to submit to the tight braces and bandages of composition; and he had, besides, too much of the gossip about him to be untinctured with the usual appurtenance of the gossip, prolixity. He was also too wise to turn or torture his natural flow of mind into a new fashion, or to apply to it any such Chinese methods of artificial restraint. Thus his characters are written with an expository diffuseness, and seem sometimes rather a commentary upon characters of the foregoing description than others of the same species. If they do not exhibit the same perpetual display of wit and coacervation of metaphor, they have much more easiness and variety, and much less stiffness and strained obscurity. They have just as much point as is necessary to render them striking, and just as much force of expression as is necessary to energize their diffuseness. They flow on enriched with many an interesting story, and many a profound reflection. Few will, we think, refuse to consider Fuller's method as the most judicious and agreeable, as his thoughts swell out to their full and healthy growth; and his illustrations receive their due modicum of relation, without being obscured by their density, or rendered rickety by their compression.

"We must now conclude our remarks on this book; and we do, in fine, most seriously recommend it to our readers, as a treasure of good sense, information, and entertainment. It is only by contrasting the works of Fuller with the lumbering and heavy productions of his contemporaries that we can properly estimate the value of the former, or give due honor to the memory of one who, in his most arduous and sterile undertakings, in the darkness of antiquities or the cloudy atmosphere of polemical divinity, never lost the vivifying spirit of his humor or the exhilarating play of his wit, or suffered his keenness of observation to be blunted by the blocks it had to work on. To him every subject was alike: if it was a dull one, he could enliven it; if it was an agreeable one, he could improve it; if it was a deep one, he could sound it; if it was a tough one, he could grapple with it. In him learning was but subsidiary to wit, and wit but secondary to wisdom; and, if his quaintness of humor gave something of the grotesque to his productions, it but added to the gloss of the admirable matter which it shone on. To him and to his pages may we always come, secure of entertainment and instruction, — of finding an agreeable olio of humorous wit and diverting sense which reciprocally relieve and play upon each other, the latter sobering and steadying the former, the former barbing and pointing the latter. In short, his works are an inexhaustible fund of sound and solid thought, — a quarry, or rather mine, of good old English heartiness, where the lighter and less elaborate artificers of modern times may seek, and seek fearlessly, for materials for their own more fragile and graceful structures.

"Of Fuller himself we can only observe, that his life was meritoriously passed, and exemplary throughout; that his opinions were independently adopted and unshrinkingly maintained. In the darkest and gloomiest period of our national history he had the sense and the wisdom to pursue the right way, and to persevere in an even tenor of moderation, as remote from interested lukewarmness as it was from mean-spirited fear. Unwilling to go all lengths with either party, he was of consequence vilified by both: willing to unite the maintainers of opposite and conflicting sentiments, he only united them against himself. Secure in the strength of his intellectual riches, the storms and hurricanes which uprooted the fabric of the constitution had only the effect of confining him more to his own resources, and of inciting him to the production of those numerous treatises and compilations for which he received from his contemporaries respect and reputation, and for which posterity will render him its tribute of unfailing gratitude."

THE HOLY STATE.

PREFACE.

TO THE READER.

WHO is not sensible with sorrow of the distractions of this age? To write books therefore may seem unseasonable, especially in a time wherein the press, like an unruly horse, hath cast off his bridle of being licensed, and some serious books, which dare fly abroad, are hooted at by a flock of pamphlets.

But be pleased to know that when I left my home it was fair weather, and my journey was half past before I discovered the tempest, and had gone so far in this work that I could neither go backward with credit nor forward with comfort.

As for the matter of this book, therein I am resident on my profession; holiness in the latitude thereof falling under the cognizance of a divine. For curious method, expect none, — essays for the most part not being placed as at a feast, but placing themselves as at an ordinary.

The characters I have conformed to the then standing laws of the realm. A twelvemonth ago were they sent to the press, since which time the wisdom of the King and State hath thought fitting to alter many things, and I expect the discretion of the reader should make his alterations accordingly. And I conjure thee by all christian ingenuity, that, if lighting here on some passages rather harsh-sounding than ill-intended, to construe the same by the general drift and main scope which is aimed at.

Nor let it render the modesty of this book suspected, because it presumes to appear in company unmanned by any patron. If right, it will defend itself; if wrong, none can defend it. Truth needs not, falsehood deserves not, a supporter. And indeed the matter of this work is too high for a subject's, the workmanship thereof too low for a prince's patronage.

And now I will turn my pen into prayer that God would be pleased to discloud these gloomy days with the beams of his mercy: which if I may be so happy as to see, it will then encourage me to count it freedom to serve two apprenticeships, — God spinning out the thick thread of my life so long, in writing the Ecclesiastical History from Christ's time to our days, if I shall from remoter parts be so planted as to enjoy the benefit of walking and standing libraries, without which advantages the best vigilance doth but vainly dream to undertake such a task.

Meantime I will stop the leakage of my soul, and what heretofore hath run out in writing shall hereafter (God willing) be improved in constant preaching, in what place soever God's providence, and friends' good will, shall fix

Thine, in all christian offices,

THOMAS FULLER.

THE HOLY STATE.

THE GOOD WIFE.

ST. PAUL to the Colossians, iii. 18, first adviseth women to submit themselves to their husbands, and then counselleth men to love their wives. And sure it was fitting that women should first have their lesson given them, because it is hardest to be learned, and therefore they need have the more time to con it. For the same reason, we first begin with the character of a good wife.

She commandeth her husband, in any equal matter, by constant obeying him. It was always observed that what the English gained of the French in battle by valor, the French regained of the English by cunning in treaties: so, if the husband should chance by his power, in his passion, to prejudice his wife's right, she wisely knoweth, by compounding and complying, to recover and rectify it again.

She never crosseth her husband in the spring-tide of his anger, but stays till it be ebbing-water. And then mildly she argues the matter, not so much to condemn him as to acquit herself. Surely, men, contrary to iron, are worse to be wrought upon when they are hot, and are far more tractable in cold blood. It is an observation of seamen, that, if a single meteor or fireball falls on their mast, it portends ill-luck; but if two come together (which they count Castor and Pollux) they presage good success: but, sure, in a family it bodeth most bad when two fireballs (husband's and wife's anger) come both together.

She keeps home, if she hath not her husband's company or leave for her patent to go abroad: for the house is the woman's centre. It is written, Psalm civ. 2: "The sun ariseth, man goeth forth unto his work, and to his labor until the evening"; but it is said of the good woman, Prov. xxxi. 15: "She riseth while it is yet night"; for man in the race of his work starts from the rising of the sun, because his business is without doors, and not to be done without the light of heaven; but the woman hath her work within the house, and therefore can make the sun rise by lighting of a candle.

Her clothes are rather comely than costly, and she makes plain cloth to be velvet by her handsome wearing it. She is none of our dainty dames, who love to appear in variety of suits every day new, — as if a good gown, like a stratagem in war, were to be used but once; but our good wife sets up a sail according to the keel of her husband's estate; and if of high parentage, she doth not so remember what she was by birth that she forgets what she is by match.

Arcana imperii (her husband's secrets) she will not divulge. Especially she is careful to conceal his infirmities. If he be none of the wisest, she so orders it that he appears on the public stage but seldom; and then he hath conned his part so well, that he comes off with great applause. If his *forma informans* be but bad, she provides him better *formas assistentes*, gets him wise servants and secretaries.

In her husband's absence, she is wife and deputy husband, which makes her double the files of her diligence. At his return he finds all things so well that he wonders to see himself at home when he was abroad.

In her husband's sickness, she feels more grief than she shows. Partly that she may not dishearten him, and partly because she is not at leisure to seem so sorrowful that she may be the more serviceable.

Her children, though many in number, are none in noise, steering them with a look whither she listeth. When they grow up, she teacheth them, not pride, but painfulness, making their hands to clothe their backs, and them to wear the livery of their own industry. She makes not her daughters gentlewomen before they be women, rather teaching them what they should pay to others than receive from them.

The heaviest work of her servants she maketh light, by orderly and seasonably enjoining it; wherefore her service is counted a preferment, and her teaching better than her wages. Her maids follow the precedent of their mistress, — live modestly at home. One asked a grave gentlewoman how her maids came by so good husbands, and yet seldom went abroad: "Oh," said she, "good husbands come home to them."

THE GOOD HUSBAND.

HAVING formerly described a good wife, she will make a good husband, whose character we are now to present.

His love to his wife weakeneth not his ruling her, and his ruling lesseneth not his loving her. Wherefore he avoideth all fondness (a sick love, to be praised in none, and pardoned only in the newly married), whereby more have wilfully betrayed their command than ever lost it by their wives' rebellion. Methinks the he-viper is right enough served, which, as Pliny reports, puts his head into the she-viper's mouth and she bites it off. And what wonder is it if women take the rule to themselves, which their uxorious husbands first surrender unto them?

He is constant to his wife, and confident of her. And, sure, where jealousy is the jailor, many break the prison, it opening more ways to wickedness than it stoppeth; so that where it findeth one it maketh ten dishonest.

He alloweth her meet maintenance, but measures it by his own estate: nor will he give less, nor can she ask more. Which allowance, if shorter than her deserts and his desire, he lengtheneth it out with his courteous carriage unto her; chiefly in her sickness, then not so much word-pitying her as providing necessaries for her.

That she may not intrench on his prerogative, he maintains her propriety in feminine affairs: yea, therein he follows her advice; for the soul of a man is planted so high that he overshoots such low matters as lie level to a woman's eye, and therefore her counsel therein may better hit the mark. Causes that are properly of feminine cognizance he suffers her finally to decide; not so much as permitting an appeal to himself, that their jurisdictions may not interfere. He will not countenance a stubborn servant against her, but in her maintains his own authority. Such husbands as bait the mistress with her maids, and clap their hands at the sport, will have cause to wring them afterwards.

Knowing she is the weaker vessel, he bears with her infirmities. All hard using of her he detests, desiring therein to do, not what may be lawful but fitting. And grant her to be of a servile nature, such as may be bettered by beating; yet he remembers he hath enfranchised her by marrying her. On her wedding-day she was, like St. Paul, free born, and privileged from any servile punishment.

He is careful that the wounds betwixt them take not air, and be not publicly known. Jars concealed are half reconciled; which, if generally known, it is a double task to stop the breach at home and men's mouths abroad. To this end he never publicly reproves her. An open reproof puts her to do penance before all that are present, after which many rather study revenge than reformation.

He keeps her in the wholesome ignorance of unnecessary secrets. They will not be starved with the ignorance, who perchance may surfeit with the knowledge of weighty counsels, too heavy for the weaker sex to bear. He knows little who will tell his wife all he knows.

He beats not his wife after his death. One

having a shrewd wife, yet loath to use her hardly in his lifetime, awed her with telling her that he would beat her when he was dead, meaning that he would leave her no maintenance. This humor is unworthy a worthy man, who will endeavor to provide her a competent estate; yet he that impoverisheth his children to enrich his widow, destroys a quick hedge to make a dead one.

THE GOOD PARENT.

HE beginneth his care for his children at their birth, giving them to God to be, if not (as Hannah did) his chaplains, at least his servants. This care he continueth till the day of his death, in their infancy, youth, and man's estate. In all which,

He showeth them in his own practice what to follow and imitate; and in others', what to shun and avoid. For though "the words of the wise be as nails fastened by the masters of the assemblies," yet sure their examples are the hammer to drive them in, to take the deeper hold. A father that whipped his son for swearing, and swore himself whilst he whipped him, did more harm by his example than good by his correction.

He doth not welcome and embrace the first

essays of sin in his children. Weeds are counted herbs in the beginning of the spring; nettles are put in pottage, and salads are made of elder-buds. Thus fond fathers like the oaths and wanton talk of their little children, and please themselves to hear them displease God. But our wise parent both instructs his children in piety, and with correction blasts the first buds of profaneness in them. He that will not use the rod on his child, his child shall be used as a rod on him.

He observeth gavel-kind in dividing his affections, though not his estate, giving each child a part. He loves them (though leaves them not) all alike. Like a well-drawn picture, he eyes all his children alike (if there be a parity of deserts), not parching one to drown another. Did not that mother show little wit in her great partiality, to whom, when her neglected son complained that his brother (her darling) had hit and hurt him with a stone, whipped him only for standing in the way where the stone went which his brother cast? This partiality is tyranny, when parents despise those that are deformed, — enough to break them whom God had bowed before.

He allows his children maintenance according to their quality; otherwise it will make them base, acquaint them with bad company and sharking tricks; and it makes them surfeit the sooner when they come to their estates. It is observed of camels, that, having travelled long without water through sandy deserts, *implentur cum bibendi est occasio et in præteritum et in futurum;* and so these thirsty heirs soak it when they come to their means, who, whilst their fathers were living, might not touch the top of his money, and think they shall never feel the bottom of it when they are dead.

In choosing a profession, he is directed by his child's disposition; whose inclination is the strongest indenture to bind him to a trade. But when they set Abel to till the ground, and send Cain to keep sheep; Jacob to hunt, and Esau to live in tents; drive some to school, and others from it; they do violence to nature, and it will thrive accordingly. Yet he humors not his child when he makes an unworthy choice beneath himself, or rather for ease than use, pleasure than profit.

If his son prove wild, he doth not cast him off so far but he marks the place where he lights. With the mother of Moses, he doth not suffer his son so to sink or swim, but he leaves one to stand afar off to watch what will become of him. He is careful whilst he quencheth his luxury, not withal to put out his life. The rather, because their souls, who have broken and run out in their youth, have proved the more healthful for it afterwards.

He moves him to marriage rather by argument drawn from his good than his own authority. It is a style too princely for a parent herein to will and command, but sure he may will and desire. Affections, like the conscience, are rather to be led than drawn.

He doth not give away his loaf to his children, and then come to them for a piece of bread. He holds the reins (though loosely) in his own hands, and keeps to reward duty and punish undutifulness; yet on good occasion, for his children's advancement, he will depart from part of his means. Base is their nature who will not have their branches lopped, till their body be felled, and will let go none of their goods as if it presaged their speedy death; whereas it doth not follow that he that puts off his cloak must presently go to bed.

On his death-bed he bequeaths his blessing to all his children; nor rejoiceth he so much to leave them great portions as honestly obtained. Only money well and lawfully gotten is good and lawful money. And if he leaves his children young, he principally nominates God to be their guardian, and next him is careful to appoint provident overseers.

THE GOOD CHILD.

HE reverenceth the person of his parent, though old, poor, and froward. As his parent bare with him when a child, he bears with his parent if twice a child; nor doth his dignity above him cancel his duty under him. When Sir Thomas More was Lord Chancellor of England, and Sir John his father one of the Judges of the King's Bench, he would in Westminster Hall beg his blessing of him on his knees.

He observes his lawful commands, and practiseth his precepts with all obedience. I cannot therefore excuse St. Barbara from undutifulness, and occasioning her own death. The matter this. Her father, being a Pagan, commanded his workmen building his house to make two windows in a room; Barbara, knowing her father's pleasure, in his absence enjoined them to make three, that seeing them she might the better contemplate the mystery of the holy trinity. (Methinks two windows might as well have raised her meditations, and the light arising from both would as properly have minded her of the Holy Spirit proceeding from the Father and the Son.) Her father, enraged at his return, thus came to the knowledge of her religion, and accused her to the magistrate, which cost her her life.

Having practised them himself, he entails his parent's precepts on his posterity. Therefore such instructions are by Solomon, Proverbs i. 9, compared to frontlets and chains (not to a suit of clothes, which serves but one, and quickly wears out, or out of fashion), which have in them a real lasting worth, and are bequeathed as legacies to another age. The same counsels observed, are chains to grace, which, neglected, prove halters to strangle undutiful children.

He is patient under correction, and thankful after it. When Mr. West, formerly Tutor (such I count *in loco parentis*) to Dr. Whitaker, was by him, then Regius Professor, created Doctor, Whitaker solemnly gave him thanks before the University for giving him correction when his young scholar.

In marriage, he first and last consults with his father; when propounded, when concluded. He best bowls at the mark of his own contentment, who, besides the aim of his own eye, is directed by his father, who is to give him the ground.

He is a stork to his parent, and feeds him in his old age: not only if his father hath been a pelican, but though he hath been an ostrich unto him, and neglected him in his youth. He confines him not a long way off to a short pension, forfeited if he comes into his presence; but shows piety at home, and learns (as St. Paul saith, 1 Timothy v. 4) to requite his parent. And yet the debt (I mean only the principal, not counting the interest) cannot fully be paid, and therefore he compounds with his father to accept in good worth the utmost of his endeavor.

Such a child God commonly rewards with long life in this world. If he chance to die young, yet he lives long that lives well; and time misspent is not lived but lost. Besides, God is better than his promise, if he takes from him a long lease, and gives him a freehold of better value. As for disobedient children,

If preserved from the gallows, they are reserved for the rack, to be tortured by their own posterity. One complained that never father had so undutiful a child as he had. "Yes," said his son, with less grace than truth, "my grandfather had."

I conclude this subject with the example of a Pagan's son, which will shame most Christians. Pomponius Atticus, making the funeral oration at the death of his mother, did protest that living with her threescore and seven years, he was never reconciled unto her, *se nunquam cum matre in gratiam rediisse:* because (take the comment with the text) there never happened betwixt them the least jar which needed reconciliation.

THE GOOD MASTER.

HE is the heart in the midst of his household, *primum vivens et ultimum moriens*, first up and last abed, if not in his person yet in his providence. In his carriage he aimeth at his own and his servants' good, and to advance both.

He oversees the works of his servants. One said that the dust that fell from the master's shoes was the best compost to manure ground. The lion out of state will not run whilst any one looks upon him; but some servants out of slothfulness will not run except some do look upon them, spurred on with their master's eye. Chiefly he is careful exactly to take his servants' reckonings. If their master takes no account of them, they will make small account of him, and care not what they spend who are never brought to an audit.

He provides them victuals, wholesome, sufficient, and seasonable. He doth not so allay his servants' bread to debase it so much as to make that servants' meat which is not man's meat. He alloweth them also convenient rest and recreation; whereas some masters, like a bad conscience, will not suffer them to sleep that have them. He remembers the old law of the Saxon King Ina, "If a villain work on

Sunday by his lord's command, he shall be free."

The wages he contracts for, he duly and truly pays to his servants. The same word in the Greek, ἰός, signifies rust and poison: and some strong poison is made of the rust of metals, but none more venomous than the rust of money in the rich man's purse, unjustly detained from the laborer, which will poison and infect his whole estate.

He never threatens his servant, but rather presently corrects him. Indeed, conditional threatenings with promise of pardon on amendment, are good and useful. Absolute threatenings torment more, reform less, making servants keep their faults, and forsake their masters: wherefore herein he never passeth his word, but makes present payment, lest the creditor run away from the debtor.

In correcting his servant, he becomes not a slave to his own passion. Not, cruelly making new indentures of the flesh of his apprentice. To this end he never beats him in the height of his passion. Moses being to fetch water out of the rock, and commanded by God only to speak to it with his rod in his hand, being transported with anger, smote it thrice. Thus some masters, which might fetch penitent tears from their servants with a chiding word (only shaking the rod withal for terror), in their fury strike many blows which might better be spared. If he perceives his servant incorrigible, so that he cannot wash the blackamoor, he washeth his hands of him, and fairly puts him away.

He is tender of his servant in his sickness and age. If crippled in his service, his house is his hospital: yet how many throw away those dry bones out of the which themselves have sucked the marrow? It is as usual to see a young serving-man an old beggar, as to see a light-horse first from the great saddle of a nobleman to come to the hackney-coach, and at last die in drawing a car. But the good master is not like the cruel hunter in the fable, who beat his old dog because his toothless mouth let go the game; he rather imitates the noble nature of our Prince Henry, who took order for the keeping of an old English mastiff which had made a lion run away. Good reason good service in age should be rewarded. Who can without pity and pleasure behold that trusty vessel which carried Sir Francis Drake about the world?

Hitherto our discourse hath proceeded of the carriage of masters towards free covenant servants, not intermeddling with their behavior towards slaves and vassals, whereof we only report this passage: When Charles the Fifth Emperor returning with his fleet from Algiers was extremely beaten with a tempest, and their ships overloaden, he caused them to cast their best horses into the sea to save the life of many slaves, which according to the market-price was not so much worth. Are there not many that in such a case had rather save Jack the horse than Jocky the keeper? And well may masters consider how easy a transposition it had been for God, to have made him to mount into the saddle that holds the stirrup; and him to sit down at the table, who stands by with a trencher.

THE GOOD SERVANT.

HE is one that out of conscience serves God in his master, and so hath the principle of obedience in himself. As for those servants who found their obedience on some external thing, with engines, they will go no longer than they are wound, or weighed up.

He doth not dispute his master's lawful will, but doeth it. Hence it is that simple servants (understand such whose capacity is bare measure, without surplusage, equal to the business he is used in) are more useful, because more manageable, than abler men, especially in matters wherein not their brains but hands are required. Yet if his master, out of want of experience, enjoins him to do what is hurtful, and prejudicial to his own estate, duty herein makes him undutiful (if not to deny, to demur in his performance), and choosing rather to displease than hurt his master, he humbly represents his reasons to the contrary.

He loves to go about his business with cheerfulness. One said, "he loved to hear his carter though not his cart to sing." God loveth a cheerful giver; and Christ reproved the Pharisees for disfiguring their faces with a sad countenance. Fools! who, to persuade men that angels lodged in their hearts, hung out a devil for a sign in their faces. Sure cheerfulness in doing renders a deed more acceptable. Not like those servants, who doing their work unwillingly, their looks do enter a protestation against what their hands are doing.

He dispatcheth his business with quickness and expedition. Hence the same English word, speed, signifies celerity, and success; the former in business of execution causing the latter. Indeed, haste and rashness are storms and tempests, breaking and wrecking business; but nimbleness is a fair full wind, blowing it with speed to the haven. As he is good at hand, so is he good at length, continually and constantly careful in his service. Many servants, as if they had learned the nature of the besoms they use, are good for a few days, and afterwards grow unserviceable.

He disposeth not of his master's goods without his privity or consent: no, not in the smallest matters. Open this wicket and it will be in vain for masters to shut the door. If servants presume to dispose small things without their master's allowance (besides that many little leaks may sink a ship), this will widen their consciences to give away greater. But though he hath not always a particular leave, he hath a general grant, and a warrant dormant from his master to give an alms to the poor in his absence, if in absolute necessity.

His answers to his master are true, direct, and dutiful. If a dumb devil possesseth a servant, a winding cane is the fittest circle, and the master the exorcist to drive it out. Some servants are so talkative, one may as well command the echo as them not to speak last; and then they count themselves conquerors, because last they leave the field. Others, though they seem to yield and go away, yet, with the flying Parthians, shoot backward over their shoulders, and dart bitter taunts at their masters; yea. though with the clock they have given the last stroke, yet they keep a jarring, muttering to themselves a good while after.

Just correction he bears patiently, and unjust he takes cheerfully; knowing that stripes unjustly given more hurt the master than the man: and the logic maxim is verified, *Agens agendo repatitur*, the smart most lights on the striker. Chiefly he disdains the baseness of running away.

Because charity is so cold, his industry is the hotter to provide something for himself, whereby he may be maintained in his old age. If under his master he trades for himself (as an apprentice may do, if he hath covenanted so beforehand), he provides good bounds and sufficient fences betwixt his own and his master's estate (Jacob, Gen. xxx. 36, set his flock three days' journey from Laban's), that no quarrel may arise about their property, nor suspicion that his remnant hath eaten up his master's whole cloth.

THE GOOD WIDOW.

SHE is a woman whose head hath been quite cut off, and yet she liveth. Conceive her to have buried her husband decently according to his quality and condition, and let us see how she behaves herself afterwards.

Her grief for her husband, though real, is moderate. Excessive was the sorrow of King Richard the Second, beseeming him neither as king, man, or Christian, who so fervently loved Anna of Bohemia his Queen, that when she died at Sheen, in Surrey, he both cursed the place, and also out of madness overthrew the whole house.

But our widow's sorrow is no storm, but a still rain. Indeed some foolishly discharge the surplusage of their passions on themselves, tearing their hair, so that their friends coming to the funeral know not which most to bemoan, the dead husband, or the dying widow. Yet commonly it comes to pass, that such widows' grief is quickly emptied, which streameth out at so large a vent; whilst their tears that but drop will hold running a long time.

She continues a competent time in her widow's estate. Anciently they were, at least, to live out their *annum luctûs*, their year of sorrow. But as some erroneously compute the long lives of the patriarchs before the flood, not by solary, but lunary years, making a month a year, so many overhasty widows cut their year of mourning very short, and within few weeks make post speed to a second marriage.

Though going abroad sometimes about her business, she never makes it her business to go abroad. Indeed "man goeth forth to his labor," and a widow in civil affairs is often forced to act a double part of man and woman, and must go abroad to solicit her business in person, what she cannot do by the proxy of her friends. Yet even then she is most careful of her credit, and tender of her modesty, not impudently thrusting into the society of men. Oh! 't is improper for tinder to strike fire, and for their sex, which are to be sued to, first to intrude and offer their company.

She loves to look on her husband's picture in the children he hath left her: not foolishly fond over them for their father's sake (this were to kill them in honor of the dead), but giveth them careful education. Her husband's friends are ever her welcomest guests, whom she entertaineth with her best cheer, and with honorable mention of their friend's and her husband's memory.

If she can speak little good of him, she speaks but little of him. So handsomely folding up her discourse that his virtues are shown outwards, and his vices wrapped up in silence, as counting it barbarism to throw dirt on his memory who hath moulds cast on his body. She is a champion for his credit, if any speak against him.

She putteth her especial confidence in God's providence. Surely if he be "a father to the fatherless," it must need follow that he is an husband to the widow. And therefore she seeks to gain and keep his love unto her, by her constant prayer and religious life.

She will not mortgage her first husband's pawns, thereby to purchase the good will of a second. If she marrieth (for which she hath the Apostle's license, not to say mandate, "I will that the younger widows marry"), she will not abridge her children of that which justly belongs unto them. Surely a broken faith to the former is but a weak foundation to build thereon a loyal affection to a latter love. Yet if she becomes a mother-in-law, there is no difference betwixt her carriage to her own and her second husband's children, save that she is severest to her own, over whom she hath the sole jurisdiction. And if her second husband's children by a former wife commit a fault, she had rather bind them over to answer for it before their own father, than to correct them herself, to avoid all suspicion of hard using of them.

THE CONSTANT VIRGIN

IS one who hath made a resolution with herself to live chaste and unmarried. Now there is a grand difference betwixt a resolution and a vow. The former is a covenant drawn up betwixt the party and herself; and commonly runs with this clause, *durante nostro beneplacito*, as long as we shall think fitting; and therefore on just occasion she may give a release to herself. But in a vow God is interested as the creditor, so that, except he be pleased to give up the bond, none can give an acquittance to themselves.

She chooseth not a single life solely for itself, but in reference to the better serving of God. A single life is none of those things to be desired in and for itself, but because it leads a more convenient way to the worshipping of God, especially in time of persecution. For then, if Christians be forced to run races for their lives, the unmarried have the advantage, lighter by many ounces, and freed from much incumbrance, which the married are subject to; who, though private persons, herein are like princes, they must have their train follow them.

She improveth her single life therewith to serve God the more constantly. Housekeepers cannot so exactly mark all their family affairs, but that sometimes their ranks will be broken; which disorder by necessary consequence will disturb their duties of piety, to make them contracted, omitted, or unseasonably performed. The Apostle saith, "Such shall have troubles in the flesh"; and grant them sanctified troubles, yet even holy-thistle and sweetbrier have their prickles. But the virgin is freed from these incumbrances. No lording husband shall at the same time command her presence and distance, to be always near in constant attendance, and always to stand aloof off in an awful observance; so that providing his breakfast hazards her soul to fast a meal of morning prayer: no crying children shall drown her singing of psalms, and put her devotion out of tune: no unfaithful servants shall force her to divide her eyes betwixt lifting them up to God and casting them down to oversee their work; but making her closet her chapel, she freely enjoyeth God and good thoughts at what time she pleaseth.

Yet in all her discourse she maketh an honorable mention of marriage. And good reason that virginity should pay a chief rent of honor unto it, as acknowledging herself to be a *colonia deducta* from it. Unworthy is the practice of those who in their discourse plant all their arguments point-blank to batter down the married estate, bitterly inveighing against it; yea, base is the behavior of some young men, who can speak nothing but satires against God's ordinance of matrimony, and the whole sex of women. This they do either out of deep dissimulation, to divert suspicion, that they may prey the farthest from their holes; or else they do it out of revenge: having themselves formerly lighted on bad women (yet no worse than they deserved), they curse all adventures because of their own shipwreck; or, lastly, they do it out of mere spite to nature and God himself: and pity it is but that their fathers had been of the same opinion. Yet it may be tolerable, if only in harmless mirth they chance to bestow a jest upon the follies of married people. Thus, when a gentlewoman told an ancient bachelor who looked very young, that she thought he had eaten a snake, "No, mistress," said he, "it is because I never meddled with any snakes which maketh me look so young."

She counts herself better lost in a modest silence than found in a bold discourse. Divinity permits not women to speak in the church; morality forbids maids to talk in the house, where their betters are present. She is far from the humors of those who (more bridling in their chins than their tongues) love in their constant prating to make sweet music to their own ears, and harsh jarring to all the rest of the company: yea, as some report of sheep, that when they run they are afraid of the noise of their own feet; so our virgin is afraid to hear her own tongue run in the presence of graver persons. She conceives the bold maintaining of any argument concludes against her own civil behavior; and yet she will give a good account of anything whereof she is questioned, sufficient to show her silence is her choice, not her refuge. In speaking, she studiously avoids all suspicious expressions, which wanton apprehensions may colorably convert into obscenity.

She blusheth at the wanton discourse of others in her company. As fearing that being in the presence where treason against modesty is spoken, all in the place will be arraigned for principal: yea, if silent, she is afraid to be taken to consent. Wherefore, that she may not suffer in her title to modesty, to preserve her right she enters a silent caveat by a blush in her cheeks, and embraceth the next opportunity to get a gaol-delivery out of that company where she was detained in durance. Now because we have mentioned blushing, which is so frequent with virgins that it is called a maiden's blush (as if they alone had a patent to dye this color), give us leave a little to enlarge ourselves on this subject.

1. Blushing oftentimes proceeds from guiltiness; when the offender, being pursued after, seeks as it were to hide himself under the vizard of a new face.

2. Blushing is other times rather a compurgator than an accuser; not arising from guiltiness in our virgin, but from one of these reasons: First, because she is surprised with a sudden accusation, and, though armed with innocency that she cannot be pierced, yet may she be amazed with so unexpected a charge. Secondly, from sensibleness of disgrace, ashamed, though innocent, to be within the suspicion of such faults, and that she hath

carried herself so that any tongue durst be so impudent as to lay it to her charge. Thirdly from a disability to acquit herself at the instant (her integrity wanting rather clearing than clearness), and perchance she wants boldness to traverse the action, and so non-suiting herself, she fears her cause will suffer in the judgments of all that be present; and although accused but in jest, she is jealous the accusation will be believed in earnest; and edged tools thrown in merriment may wound reputations. Fourthly, out of mere anger; for as in fear the blood makes not an orderly retreat, but a confused flight to the heart, so in blushing the blood sallies out into our virgin's cheeks, and seems as a champion to challenge the accuser for wronging her.

3. Where small faults are committed, blushing obtains a pardon of course with ingenuous beholders. As if she be guilty of casual incivilities, or solecisms in manners occasioned by invincible ignorance and unavoidable mistakes, in such a case blushing is a sufficient penance to restore her to her state of innocency.

She imprisons not herself with a solemn vow never to marry. For none know their own strength herein. Who hath sailed about the world of his own heart, sounded each creek, surveyed each corner, but that still there remains therein much *terra incognita* to himself? Junius, at the first little better than a misogynist, was afterwards so altered from himself that he successively married four wives.

As she lives with less care, so she dies with more cheerfulness. Indeed, she was rather a sojourner than an inhabitant in this world, and therefore forsakes it with the less grief. In a word, the way to heaven is alike narrow to all estates, but far smoother to the virgin than to the married.

THE ELDER BROTHER

IS one who made haste to come into the world to bring his parents the first news of male posterity, and is well rewarded for his tidings.

He is thankful for the advantage God gave him at the starting in the race into this world. When twins have been even matched, one hath gained the goal but by his length. St. Augustine saith, that it is every man's bounden duty solemnly to celebrate his birthday. If so, elder brothers may best afford good cheer on the festival.

He counts not his inheritance a writ of ease to free him from industry ; as if only the younger brothers came into the world to work, the elder to compliment. These are the tops of their houses indeed, like cotlofts, highest and emptiest. Rather he laboreth to furnish himself with all gentle accomplishments, being best able to go to the cost of learning. He need not fear to be served as Ulrich Fugger was (chief of the noble family of the Fuggers in Augsburg), who was disinherited of a great patrimony only for his studiousness, and expensiveness in buying costly manuscripts.

He doth not so remember he is an heir, that he forgets he is a son. Wherefore his carriage to his parents is always respectful. It may chance that his father may be kept in a charitable prison, whereof his son hath the keys; the old man being only tenant for life, and the lands entailed on our young gentleman. In such a case, when it is in his power, if necessity requires, he enlargeth his father to such a reasonable proportion of liberty as may not be injurious to himself.

He rather desires his father's life than his living.

His father's deeds and grants he ratifies and confirms. If a stitch be fallen in a lease, he will not widen it into an hole by cavilling, till the whole strength of the grant run out thereat; or take advantage of the default of the clerk in the writing where the deed appears really done, and on a valuable consideration. He counts himself bound in honor to perform what by marks and signs he plainly understands his father meant, though he spake it not out.

He reflecteth his lustre to grace and credit his younger brethren. Thus Scipio Africanus, after his great victories against the Carthaginians and conquering of Hannibal, was content to serve as a lieutenant in the wars of Asia, under Lucius Scipio his younger brother.

He relieveth his distressed kindred, yet so as he continues them in their calling. Otherwise they would all make his house their hospital, his kindred their calling. When one being an husbandman challenged kindred of Robert Grosthead, Bishop of Lincoln, and thereupon requested favor of him to bestow an office on him, "Cousin," quoth the Bishop, "if your cart be broken, I'll mend it; if your plough old, I'll give you a new one, and seed to sow your land; but an husbandman I found you and an husbandman I'll leave you." It is better to ease poor kindred in their profession than to ease them from their profession.

He is careful to support the credit and dignity of his family; neither wasting his paternal estate by his unthriftiness, nor marring it by parcelling his ancient manors and demesnes amongst his younger children, whom he provides for by annuities, pensions, moneys, leases, and purchased lands. He remembers how, when our King Alfred divided the river of Lee (which parts Hertfordshire and Essex) into three streams, it became so shallow that boats could not row where formerly ships did ride. Thus the ancient family of the Woodfords (which had long continued in Leicestershire and elsewhere in England in great account, estate, and livelihood) is at this day quite extinct. For when Sir Thomas Woodford, in the reign of King Henry the Sixth, made almost an even partition of his means betwixt his five grandchildren, the house in short space utterly decayed; not any part of his lands now in the tenure or name of any of his male line, some whereof lived to be brought to a low ebb of fortune. Yet, on the other side, to leave all to the eldest and make no provision for the rest of their children, is against all rules of religion, forgetting their Christian name to remember their surname.

THE YOUNGER BROTHER.

SOME account him the better gentleman of the two because son to the more ancient gentleman. Wherein his elder brother can give him the hearing, and a smile into the bargain. He shares equally with his elder brother in the education, but differs from him in his portion; and though he giveth also his father's arms, yet, to use the Herald's language, he may say, —

> "This to my elder brother I must yield,
> I have the charge, but he hath all the field."

Like herein to a young nephew of Tarquin's in Rome, who was called Egereus, from wanting of maintenance because his grandfather left him nothing. It was therefore a mannerly answer which a young gentleman gave to King James when he asked him what kin he was to such a lord of his name. "Please your Majesty," said he, "my elder brother is his cousin-german."

He repines not at the providence of God in ordering his birth. Heirs are made, even where matches are, both in heaven. Even in twins, God will have one next the door to come first into the world.

He labors by his endeavors to date himself an elder brother. Nature makes but one, industry doth make all the sons of the same man heirs. The fourth brother gives a martilet for the difference of his arms, a bird observed to build either in castles, steeples, or ships; showing that the bearer hereof, being debarred from all hopes of his father's inheritance, must seek by war, learning, or merchandise to advance his estate.

In war, he cuts out his fortunes with his own sword. William the Conqueror, when he first landed his forces in England, burnt all his ships, that despair to return might make his men the more valiant. Younger brothers, being cut off at home from all hopes, are more zealous to purchase an honorable support abroad. Their small arteries with great spirits have wrought miracles, and their resolution hath driven success before it. Many of them have adventured to cheapen dear enterprises, and were only able to pay the earnest; yet fortune hath accepted them for chapmen, and hath freely forgiven them the rest of the payment for their boldness.

Nor are they less happy if applying themselves to their book; nature generally giving them good wits, which, because they want room to burnish, may the better afford to soar high.

But he gaineth more wealth if betaking himself to merchandise; whence often he riseth to the greatest annual honor in the kingdom. Many families in England, though not first raised from the city, yet thence have been so restored and enriched that it may seem to amount to an original raising. Neither doth an apprenticeship extinguish native nor disenable to acquisitive gentry; and they are much mistaken who hold it to be in the nature of bondage. For, first, his indenture is a civil contract, whereof a bondman is uncapable; secondly, (no work can be base prescribed in reference to a noble end) as theirs is that learn an honest mystery to enable them for the service of God and the country; thirdly, they give round sums of money to be bound. Now, if apprenticeship be a servitude, it is either a pleasing bondage, or strange madness to purchase it at so dear a rate. Gentry therefore may be suspended perchance, and sleep during the apprenticeship, but it awakens afterwards.

Sometimes he lighteth on a wealthy match to advance him; if meeting with one that is pilot of her own affections, to steer them without guidance of her friends, and such as disdaineth her marriage should be contracted in an exchange where jointure must weigh every grain even to the portion. Rather she counts it an act both of love and charity to affect one rich in deserts, who commonly hath the advantage of birth as she hath of means; and so it is made level betwixt them. And thus many a young gentleman hath gotten honorable maintenance by an heiress.

His means the more hardly gotten are the more carefully kept. Heat gotten by degrees, with motion and exercise, is more natural and stays longer by one than what is gotten all at once by coming to the fire. Goods acquired by industry prove commonly more lasting than lands by descent.

He ever owneth his elder brother with dutiful respect; yea, though God should so bless his endeavors as to go beyond him in wealth and honor. The pride of the Jesuits is generally taxed, who, being the youngest of all other orders, and therefore by canon to go last, will never go in procession with other orders, because they will not come behind them.

Sometimes the paternal inheritance falls to them who never hoped to rise to it. Thus John, surnamed Sans-terre, or Without-land, having five elder brothers, came to the kingdom of England, death levelling those which stood betwixt him and the crown. It is observed of the Coringtons, an ancient family in Cornwall, that, for eight lineal descents, never any one that was born heir had the land, but it ever fell to younger brothers.

To conclude, there is a hill in Voitland (a small country in Germany) called Feitchtelberg, out of which arise four rivers running four several ways, viz: 1. Eger, east; 2. Menus, west; 3. Sala, north; and 4. Nabus, south: so that he that sees their fountains so near together would admire at their falls so far asunder. Thus the younger sons of the same mother and father, embracing different courses to try their fortunes abroad in the world, chance often to die far off, at great distance, which were all born in the same place.

—♦—

THE GOOD ADVOCATE.

HE is one that will not plead that cause wherein his tongue must be confuted by his conscience. It is the praise of the Spanish soldier that, whilst all other nations are mercenary and for money will serve on any side, he will never fight against his own king; nor will our advocate against the sovereign truth plainly appearing to his conscience.

He not only hears but examines his client, and pincheth the cause where he fears it is foundered. For many clients in telling their case rather plead than relate it, so that the advocate hears not the true state of it till opened by the adverse party. Surely the lawyer that fills himself with instructions will travel longest in the cause without tiring. Others that are so quick in searching, seldom search to the quick; and those miraculous apprehensions who understand more than all before the client had told half, run without their errand and will return without their answer.

If the matter be doubtful, he will only warrant his own diligence. Yet some keep an assurance-office in their chamber, and will warrant any cause brought unto them, as knowing that, if they fail, they lose nothing but what long since was lost, their credit.

He makes not a Trojan siege of a suit, but seeks to bring it to a set battle in a speedy trial. Yet sometimes suits are continued by their difficulty, the potency and stomach of the parties, without any default in the lawyer.

He is faithful to the side that first retains him. Not like Demosthenes, who secretly wrote one oration for Phormio, and another in the same matter for Apollodorus, his adversary.

In pleading he shoots fairly at the head of the cause, and having fastened, no frowns nor favors shall make him let go his hold. Not snatching aside here and there to no purpose, speaking little in much, as it was said of Anaximenes, "that he had a flood of words and a drop of reason." His boldness riseth or falleth as he apprehends the goodness or badness of his cause.

He joys not to be retained in such a suit where all the right in question is but a drop blown up with malice to be a bubble. Wherefore, in such trivial matters, he persuades his client to sound a retreat and make a composition.

When his name is up, his industry is not down, thinking to plead not by his study but his credit. Commonly, physicians, like beer, are best when they are old; and lawyers, like bread, when they are young and new. But our advocate grows not lazy; and if a leading case be out of the road of his practice, he will take pains to trace it through his books, and prick the footsteps thereof wheresoever he finds it.

He is more careful to deserve, than greedy to take, fees. He accounts the very pleading of a poor widow's honest cause sufficient fees, as conceiving himself then the King of Heaven's advocate, bound *ex officio* to prosecute it. And although some may say that such a lawyer may even go live in Cornwall, where it is observed that few of that profession hitherto have grown to any great livelihood, yet shall he, besides those two felicities of common lawyers, that they seldom die either without heirs or making a will, find God's blessing on his provisions and posterity.

THE GOOD JUDGE.

THE good advocate whom we formerly described is since, by his prince's favor and own deserts, advanced to be a judge; which his place he freely obtained with Sir Augustine Nicolls, whom King James used to call "the judge that would give no money." Otherwise they that buy justice by wholesale, to make themselves savers, must sell it by retail.

He is patient and attentive in hearing the pleadings on both sides, and hearkens to the witnesses, though tedious. He may give a waking testimony who hath but a dreaming utterance; and many country people must be impertinent before they can be pertinent, and cannot give evidence about a hen but first they must begin with it in the egg. All which our judge is contented to hearken to.

He meets not a testimony half-way, but stays till it come at him. He that proceeds on half-evidence will not do quarter-justice. Our judge will not go till he is led. If any shall browbeat a pregnant witness on purpose to make his proof miscarry, he checketh them and helps the witness that labors in his delivery. On the other side, he nips those lawyers who, under a pretence of kindness to lend a witness some words, give him new matter, yea, clean contrary to what he intended.

Having heard with patience, he gives sentence with uprightness. For when he put on his robes he put off his relations to any, and, like Melchisedech, becomes without pedigree.

His private affections are swallowed up in the common cause, as rivers lose their names in the ocean. He therefore allows no noted favorites, which cannot but cause multiplication of fees and suspicion of by-ways.

He silences that lawyer who seeks to set the neck of a bad cause, once broken with a definitive sentence; and causeth that contentious suits be spewed out, as the surfeits of courts.

He so hates bribes that he is jealous to receive any kindness above the ordinary proportion of friendship; lest, like the sermons of wandering preachers, they should end in begging. And, surely, integrity is the proper portion of a judge. Men have a touchstone whereby to try gold; but gold is the touchstone whereby to try men. It was a shrewd gird which Catulus gave the Roman judge for acquitting Clodius, a great malefactor, when he met them going home well attended with officers: "You do well," quoth he, "to be well guarded for your safety, lest the money be taken away from you, you took for bribes." Our judge also detesteth the trick of mendicant friars, who will touch no money themselves, but have a boy with a bag to receive it for them.

When he sits upon life, in judgment he remembereth mercy. Then (they say) a butcher may not be of the jury, much less let him be the judge. Oh let him take heed how he strikes that hath a dead hand. It was the charge Queen Mary gave to Judge Morgan, chief justice of the common pleas, that, notwithstanding the old error amongst judges did not admit any witness to speak or any other matter to be heard in favor of the adversary, her Majesty being party, yet her Highness' pleasure was, that whatsoever could be brought in the favor of the subject should be admitted and heard.

If the cause be difficult, his diligence is the greater to sift it out. For though there be mention, Psalm xxxvii. 6, of "righteousness as clear as the noonday," yet God forbid that that innocency which is no clearer than twilight should be condemned. And seeing one's oath commands another's life, he searcheth whether malice did not command that oath; yet when all is done, the judge may be deceived by false evidence. But blame not the hand of the dial if it points at a false hour, when the fault is in the wheels of the clock which direct it and are out of frame.

The sentence of condemnation he pronounceth with all gravity. It is best when steeped in the judge's tears. He avoideth all jesting on men in misery; easily may he put them out of countenance whom he hath power to put out of life.

Such as are unworthy to live and yet unfitted to die, he provides shall be instructed. By God's mercy and good teaching, the reprieve of their bodies may get the pardon of their souls, and one day's longer life for them here may procure a blessed eternity for them hereafter, as may appear by this memorable example. It happened about the year one thousand five hundred and fifty-six, in the town of Weissenstein, in Germany, that a Jew, for theft he had committed, was in this cruel manner to be executed: he was hanged by the feet with his head downwards betwixt two dogs, which constantly snatched and bit at him. The strangeness of the torment moved Jacobus Andreas, a grave, moderate, and learned divine as any in that age, to go to behold it. Coming thither, he found the poor wretch, as he hung, repeating verses out of the Hebrew Psalms, wherein he cried out to God for mercy. Andreas hereupon took occasion to counsel him to trust in Jesus Christ, the true Saviour of mankind. The Jew embracing the Christian faith requested but this one thing, — that he might be taken down and be baptized, though presently after he were hanged again, (but by the neck, as Christian malefactors suffered,) which was accordingly granted him.

He is exact to do justice in civil suits betwixt sovereign and subject. This will most ingratiate him with his prince at last. Kings neither are, can, nor should be lawyers themselves by reason of higher state employments; but herein they see with the eyes of their judges, and at last will break those false spectacles which in point of law shall be found to have deceived them.

He counts the rules of state and the laws of the realm mutually support each other. Those who made the laws to be not only disparate, but even opposite terms to maxims of government, were true friends neither to laws nor government. Indeed, *salus reipublicæ* is *charta maxima:* extremity makes the next the best remedy. Yet though hot waters be good to be given to one in a swoon, they will burn his heart out who drinks them constantly when in health. Extraordinary courses are not ordinarily to be used when not enforced by absolute necessity.

And thus we leave our good judge to receive a just reward of his integrity from the Judge of judges at the great assize of the world.

THE GOOD PHYSICIAN.

COMING to his patient, he persuades him to put his trust in God, the fountain of health. The neglect hereof hath caused the bad success of the best physicians; for God will manifest that, though skill come mediately from him, to be gotten by man's pains, success comes from him immediately, to be disposed at his pleasure.

He hansels not his new experiments on the bodies of his patients; letting loose mad receipts into the sick man's body, to try how well nature in him will fight against them, whilst himself stands by and sees the battle; except it be in desperate cases, when death must be expelled by death.

To poor people he prescribes cheap but wholesome medicine; not removing the consumption out of their bodies into their purses; nor sending them to the East Indies for drugs when they can reach better out of their gardens.

Lest his apothecary should oversee, he oversees his apothecary. For though many of that profession be both able and honest, yet some, out of ignorance or haste, may mistake: — witness one of Blois, who, being to serve a doctor's bill, instead of *optimi* (short written) read *opii*, and had sent the patient asleep to his grave if the doctor's watchfulness had not prevented him. Worse are those who make wilful errors, giving one thing for another. A prodigal, who had spent his estate, was pleased to jeer himself, boasting that he had cozened those who had bought his means. "They gave me," said he, "good new money, and I sold them my great-great-grandfather's old land." But this cozenage is too true in many apothecaries, selling to sick folk for new money antiquated drugs, and making dying men's physic of dead ingredients.

He brings not news, with a false spy, that the coast is clear, till death surprises the sick man. I know, physicians love to make the best of their patient's estate. First, it is improper that *adjutores vitæ* should be *nuncii mortis*. Secondly, none, with their good will, will tell bad news. Thirdly, their fee may be the worse for it. Fourthly, 't is a confessing that their art is conquered. Fifthly, it will poison their patient's heart with grief and make it break before the time. However, they may so order it that the party may be informed of his dangerous condition, that he be not outed of this world before he be provided for another.

When he can keep life no longer in, he makes a fair and easy passage for it to go out. He giveth his attendance for the facilitating and assuaging of the pains and agonies of death. Yet, generally, 't is death to a physician to be with a dying man.

Unworthy pretenders to physic are rather foils than stains to the profession. Such a one was that counterfeit who called himself the Baron of Blackamore, and feigned he was sent from the Emperor to our young King Henry the Sixth, to be his principal physician; but his forgery being discovered, he was apprehended, and executed in the Tower of London, *anno* 1426; and such the world daily swarms with. Well did the poets feign Æsculapius and Circe, brother and sister, and both children of the Sun; for in all times, in the opinion of the multitude, witches, old women, and impostors have had a competition with physicians. And commonly the most ignorant are the most confident in their undertakings, and will not stick to tell you what disease the gall of a dove is good to cure. He took himself to be no mean doctor, who, being guilty of no Greek, and being demanded why it was called an "hectic fever"; "because," saith he, "of an hecking cough, which ever attendeth that disease."

THE FAITHFUL MINISTER.

WE suppose him not brought up by hand only in his own country studies, but that he hath suck of his Mother University, and thoroughly learnt the arts; not as St. Rumball, who is said to have spoken as soon as he was born, doth he preach as soon as he is matriculated. Conceive him now a graduate in arts and called to a pastoral charge, and then let us see how well he dischargeth his office.

He endeavors to get the general love and good-will of his parish. This he doth not so much to make a benefit of them, as a benefit for them, that his ministry may be more effectual; otherwise he may preach his own heart out before he preacheth anything into theirs. The good conceit of the physician is half a cure, and his practice will scarce be happy where his person is hated; yet he humors them not in his doctrine to get their love, for such a spaniel is worse than a dumb dog. He shall sooner get their good-will by walking uprightly than by crouching and creeping. If pious living and painful laboring in his calling will not win their affections, he counts it gain to lose them. As for those which causelessly hate him, he pities and prays for them; and such there will be. I should suspect his preaching had no salt in it, if no galled horse did wince.

He is strict in ordering his conversation. As for those who cleanse blurs with blotted fingers, they make it the worse. It was said of one who preached very well and lived very ill, that "when he was out of the pulpit it was pity he should ever go into it, and when he was in the pulpit it was pity he should ever come out of it"; but our minister lives sermons. And yet I deny not but dissolute men, like unskilful horsemen which open a gate on the wrong side, may by the virtue of their office open heaven for others and shut themselves out.

His behavior towards his people is grave and courteous; not too austere and retired, which is laid to the charge of good Mr. Hooper the martyr, that his rigidness frighted people from consulting with him. "Let your light," saith Christ, "shine before men"; whereas over-reservedness makes the brightest virtue burn dim. Especially he detesteth affected gravity (which is rather on men than in them), whereby some belie their register-book, antedate their age to seem far older than they are, and plait and set their brows in an affected sadness. Whereas St. Anthony, the monk, might have been known among hundreds of his order by his cheerful face, he having ever, though a most mortified man, a merry countenance.

He doth not clash God's ordinances together about precedency; not making odious comparisons betwixt prayer and preaching, preaching and catechizing, public prayer and private, premeditate prayer and extempore. When, at the taking of New Carthage, in Spain, two soldiers contended about the mural crown, due to him who first climbed the walls, so that the whole army was thereupon in danger of division, Scipio, the General, said, "he knew that they both got up the wall together," and so gave the scaling crown to them both. Thus our minister compounds all controversies betwixt God's ordinances by praising them all, practising them all, and thanking God for them all.

He carefully catechizeth his people in the elements of religion; except he hath (a rare thing) a flock without lambs, — all of old sheep; and yet even Luther did not scorn to profess himself *discipulum catechismi*, a scholar of the catechism. By this catechizing, the Gospel first got ground of Popery; and let not our religion, now grown rich, be ashamed of that which first gave it credit and set it up, lest the Jesuits beat us at our own weapon. Through the want of this catechizing, many which are well skilled in some dark out-corners of divinity have lost themselves in the beaten road thereof.

He will not offer to God of that which costs him nothing, but takes pains aforehand for his sermons. Demosthenes never made any oration on the sudden; yea, being called upon, he never rose up to speak except he had well studied the matter; and he was wont to say that he showed how he honored and reverenced the people of Athens, because he was careful what he spake unto them. Indeed, if our minister be surprised with a sudden occasion, he counts himself rather to be excused than commended, if, premeditating only the bones of his sermon, he clothes it with flesh extempore. As for those whose long custom hath made preaching their nature that they can discourse sermons without study, he accounts their examples rather to be admired than imitated.

Having brought his sermon into his head, he labors to bring it into his heart before he preaches it to his people. Surely, that preaching which comes from the soul most works on the soul. Some have questioned ventriloquy, when men strangely speak out of their bellies, whether it can be done lawfully or no; might I coin the word cordiloquy, when men draw the doctrines out of their hearts, sure all would count this lawful and commendable.

He chiefly reproves the reigning sins of the time and place he lives in. We may observe that our Saviour never inveighed against idolatry, usury, sabbath-breaking, amongst the Jews; not that these were not sins, but they were not practised so much in that age, wherein wickedness was spun with a finer thread; and therefore Christ principally bent the drift of his preaching against spiritual pride, hypocrisy, and traditions, then predominant amongst the people. Also our minister confuteth no old heresies which time hath confuted; nor troubles his auditory with such strange, hideous cases of conscience, that it is more hard to find the case than the resolution. In public reproving of sin he ever whips the vice and spares the person.

He doth not only move the bread of life and toss it up and down in generalities, but also breaks it into particular directions, drawing it down to cases of conscience that a man may be warranted in his particular actions whether they be lawful or not. And he teacheth people their lawful liberty as well as their restraints and prohibitions ; for amongst men it is as ill taken to turn back favors as to disobey commands.

The places of scripture he quotes are pregnant and pertinent. As for heaping up of many quotations it smacks of a vain ostentation of memory. Besides it is as impossible that the hearer should profitably retain them all, as that the preacher had seriously perused them all; yea, whilst the auditors stop their attention and stoop down to gather an impertinent quotation, the sermon runs on and they lose more substantial matter.

His similes and illustrations are always familiar, never contemptible. Indeed, reasons are the pillars of the fabric of a sermon, but similitudes are the windows which give the best lights. He avoids such stories whose mention may suggest bad thoughts to the auditors, and will not use a light comparison to make thereof a grave application, for fear lest his poison go farther than his antidote.

He provideth not only wholesome but plentiful food for his people. Almost incredible was the painfulness of Baronius, the compiler of the voluminous annals of the church, who, for thirty years together, preached three or four times a week to the people. As for our minister, he preferreth rather to entertain his people with wholesome cold meat which was on the table before, than with that which is hot from the spit, raw and half roasted. Yet, in repetition of the same sermon, every edition hath a new addition, if not of new matter, of new affections. "Of whom," saith St. Paul, "we have told you often, and now we tell you weeping."

He makes not that wearisome, which should ever be welcome. Wherefore his sermons are of an ordinary length, except on an extraordinary occasion. What a gift had John Halsebach, Professor at Vienna, in tediousness? who, being to expound the Prophet Esay to his auditors, read twenty-one years on the first chapter, and yet finished it not.

He counts the success of his ministry the greatest preferment. Yet herein God hath humbled many painful pastors, in making them to be clouds to rain, not over Arabia the Happy, but over the Stony or Desert: so that they may complain with the herdsman in the poet,

> "Heu mihi, quàm pingui macer est mihi taurus in arvo!"
>
> My starveling bull,
> Ah wo is me,
> In pasture full,
> How lean is he!

Yet such pastors may comfort themselves that great is their reward with God in heaven, who measures it not by their success but endeavors. Besides, though they see not, their people may feel benefit by their ministry. Yea, the preaching of the word in some places is like the planting of woods, where, though no profit is received for twenty years together, it comes afterwards. And grant that God honors thee not to build his temple in thy parish, yet thou mayest with David provide metal and materials for Solomon thy successor to build it with.

To sick folks he comes sometimes before he is sent for, as counting his vocation a sufficient calling. None of his flock shall want the extreme unction of prayer and counsel. Against the communion, especially, he endeavors that Janus's temple be shut in the whole parish, and that all be made friends.

He is never plaintiff in any suit but to be right's defendant. If his dues be detained from him, he grieves more for his parishioners' bad consciences than his own damage. He had rather suffer ten times in his profit than once in his title, where not only his person, but posterity is wronged: and then he proceeds fairly and speedily to a trial, that he may not vex and weary others, but right himself. During his suit, he neither breaks off nor slacks offices of courtesy to his adversary; yea, though he loseth his suit, he will not also lose his charity.

He is moderate in his tenets and opinions. Not that he gilds over lukewarmness in matters of moment with the title of discretion, but withal he is careful not to entitle violence in indifferent and inconcerning matters to be zeal. Indeed, men of extraordinary tallness (though otherwise little deserving) are made porters to lords; and those of unusual littleness are made ladies' dwarfs, whilst men of moderate stature may want masters. Thus, many notorious for extremities may find favorers to prefer them, whilst moderate men in the middle truth may want any to advance them. But what saith the apostle? "If in this life only we had hope, we are of all men the most miserable."

He is sociable and willing to do any courtesy for his neighbor ministers. He willingly communicates his knowledge unto them. Surely the gifts and graces of Christians lay in common, till base envy made the first enclosure. He neither slighteth his inferiors nor repineth at those who in parts and credit are above him. He loveth the company of his neighbor ministers. Sure as ambergris is nothing so sweet in itself as when it is compounded with other things, so both godly and learned men are gainers by communicating themselves to their neighbors.

He is careful in the discreet ordering of his own family. A good minister and a good father may well agree together. When a certain Frenchman came to visit Melancthon, he found him in his stove, with one hand dandling his child, and in the other hand holding a book and reading it. Our minister also is as hospitable as his estate will permit, and makes every alms two by his cheerful giving it. He loveth also to live in a well-repaired house, that he may serve God therein more cheerfully. A clergyman who built his house from the ground wrote in it this counsel to his successor: —

"If thou dost find an house built to thy mind
Without thy cost,
Serve thou the more God and the poor;
My labor is not lost."

Lying on his deathbed, he bequeaths to each of his parishioners his precepts and example for a legacy; and they in requital erect every one a monument for him in their hearts. He is so far from that base jealousy that his memory should be outshined by a brighter successor, and from that wicked desire that his people may find his worth by the worthlessness of him that succeeds, that he doth heartily pray to God to provide them a better pastor after his decease. As for outward estate, he commonly lives in too bare pasture to die fat: it is well if he hath gathered any flesh, being more in blessing than bulk.

THE CONTROVERSIAL DIVINE.

HE is truth's champion, to defend her against all adversaries, atheists, heretics, schismatics, and erroneous persons whatsoever. His sufficiency appears in opposing, answering, moderating, and writing.

He engageth both his judgment and affections in opposing of falsehood. Not like country fencers, who play only to make sport, but like duellers indeed, as if for life and limb; chiefly if the question be of large prospect and great concernings, he is zealous in the quarrel. Yet some, though their judgment weigh down on one side, the beam of their affections stands so even, they care not which part prevails.

In opposing a truth, he dissembles himself her foe, to be her better friend. Wherefore he counts himself the greatest conqueror when truth hath taken him captive. With Joseph, having sufficiently sifted the matter in a disguise, he discovereth himself, "I am Joseph your brother," and then throws away his vizard. Dishonest they, who, though the debt be satisfied, will never give up the bond, but continue wrangling when the objection is answered.

He abstains from all foul and railing language. What? make the muses, yea, the graces scolds? Such purulent spittle argues exulcerated lungs. Why should there be so much railing about the body of Christ, when there was none about the body of Moses in the act kept betwixt the devil and Michael the archangel?

He tyrannizeth not over a weak and undermatched adversary; but seeks rather to cover his weakness, if he be a modest man. When a Professor pressed an answerer (a better Christian than a clerk) with a hard argument,—*Reverende Professor*, said he, *ingenue confiteor me non posse respondere huic argumento.* To whom the Professor,— *Recte respondes.*

In answering, he states the question, and expoundeth the terms thereof. Otherwise the disputants shall end, where they ought to have begun, in differences about words, and be barbarians each to other, speaking in a language neither understands. If the question also be of historical cognizance, he shows the pedigree thereof, who first brewed it, who first broached it, and sends the wandering error with a passport home to the place of its birth.

In taking away an objection, he not only puts by the thrust, but breaks the weapon. Some rather escape than defeat an argument; and though, by such an evasion, they may shut the mouth of the opponent, yet may they open the difficulty wider in the hearts of the hearers. But our answerer either fairly resolves the doubt, or else shows the falseness of the argument, by beggaring the opponent to maintain such a fruitful generation of absurdities as his argument hath begotten; or, lastly, returns and retorts it back upon him again. The first way unties the knot; the second cuts it asunder; the third whips the opponent with the knot himself tied. Sure, 't is more honor to be a clear answerer than a cunning opposer, because the latter takes advantage of man's ignorance, which is ten times more than his knowledge.

What his answers want in suddenness, they have in solidity. Indeed, the speedy answer adds lustre to the disputation, and honor to the disputant; yet he makes good payment, who, though he cannot presently throw the money out of his pocket, yet will pay it, if but going home to unlock his chest. Some that are not for speedy may be for sounder performance.

When Melancthon, at the disputation of Ratisbon, was pressed with a shrewd argument by Eckius, "I will answer thee," said he, "to-morrow." "Nay," said Eckius, "do it now, or it is nothing worth." "Yea," said Melancthon, "I seek the truth, and not mine own credit, and therefore it will be as good if I answer thee to-morrow by God's assistance."

In moderating, he sides with the answerer, if the answerer sides with the truth. But if he be conceited, and opinioned of his own sufficiency, he lets him swoon before he gives him any hot water. If a paradox-monger, loving to hold strange, yea, dangerous opinions, he counts it charity to suffer such a one to be beaten without mercy, that he may be weaned from his wilfulness. For the main, he is so a staff to the answerer, that he makes him stand on his own legs.

In writing, his Latin is pure, so far as the subject will allow; for those who are to climb the Alps are not to expect a smooth and even way. True it is, that schoolmen, perceiving that fallacy had too much covert under the nap of flourishing language, used threadbare Latin on purpose, and cared not to trespass on grammar, and tread down the fences thereof to avoid the circuit of words, and to go the nearest way to express their conceits. But our divine, though he useth barbarous school-terms, which, like standers, are fixed to the controversy, yet, in his movable Latin, passages, and digressions, his style is pure and elegant.

He affects clearness and plainness in all his writings. Some men's heads are like the world before God said unto it, *Fiat lux.* These dark lanterns may shine to themselves, and understand their own conceits, but nobody else can have light from them. Thus Matthias Farinator, Professor at Vienna, assisted with some other learned men, as the times then went, was thirty years making a book of applying Plato's, Aristotle's, and Galen's rules in philosophy, to Christ and his Prophets, and 't is called *lumen animæ; quo tamen nihil est caliginosius, labore magno, sed ridiculo et inani.* But this obscurity is worst when affected, when they do as Persius, of whom one saith,—*Legi voluit quæ scripsit, intelligi noluit quæ legerentur.* Some affect this darkness, that they may be accounted profound, whereas one is not bound to believe that all the water is deep that is muddy.

He is not curious in searching matters of no moment. Captain Martin Frobisher fetched from the farthest northern countries a ship's lading of mineral stones, as he thought, which afterwards were cast out to mend the highways. Thus are they served, and miss their hopes, who, long seeking to extract hidden mysteries out of nice questions, leave them off as useless at last. Antoninus Pius, for his desire to search to the least differences, was called *cumini sector*, the carver of cumin seed. One need not be so accurate; for as soon shall one scour the spots out of the moon, as all ignorance out of man. When Eunomius the heretic vaunted that he knew God and his divinity, St. Basil gravels him in twenty-one questions about the body of an ant or pismire; so dark is man's understanding. I wonder, therefore, at the boldness of some, who, as if they were Lord Marshals of the angels, place them in ranks and files. Let us not believe them here, but rather go to heaven to confute them.

He neither multiplies needless, nor compounds necessary controversies. Sure they light on a labor in vain who seek to make a bridge of reconciliation over the μέγα χάσμα betwixt Papists and Protestants; for though we go ninety-nine steps, they (I mean their Church) will not come one, to give us a meeting. And as for the offers of Clara's and private men, (besides that they seem to be more of the nature of baits than gifts,) they may make large proffers, without any commission to treat, and so the Romish Church not bound to pay their promises. In Merionethshire, in Wales, there are high mountains, whose hanging tops come so close together that shepherds on the tops of several hills may audibly talk together, yet will it be a day's journey for their bodies to meet, so vast is the hollowness of the vallies betwixt them. Thus, upon sound search shall we find a grand distance and remoteness betwixt Popish and Protestant tenets to reconcile them, which, at the first view, may seem near, and tending to an accommodation.

He is resolute and stable in fundamental points of religion. These are his fixed poles and axle-tree, about which he moves, whilst they stand unmoveable. Some sail so long on the sea of controversies, tossed up and down, to and fro, *pro* and *con*, that the very ground to them seems to move, and their judgments grow skeptical and unstable in the most settled points of divinity. When he cometh to preach, especially if to a plain auditory, with the Paracelsians he extracts an oil out of the driest and hardest bodies; and, knowing that knotty timber is unfit to build with, he edifies people with easy and profitable matter.

THE TRUE CHURCH ANTIQUARY.

HE is a traveller into former times, whence he hath learnt their language and fashions. If he meets with an old manuscript, which hath the mark worn out of its mouth, and hath lost the date, yet he can tell the age thereof, either by the phrase or character.

He baits at middle antiquity, but lodges not till he comes at that which is ancient indeed. Some scour off the rust of old inscriptions into their own souls, cankering themselves with superstition, having read so often, *Orate pro anima*, that at last they fall a-praying for the departed; and they more lament the ruin of monasteries than the decay and ruin of monks' lives, degenerating from their ancient piety and painfulness. Indeed, a little skill in antiquity inclines a man to popery; but depth in that study brings him about again to our religion. A nobleman who had heard of the extreme age of one dwelling not far off, made a journey to visit him, and finding an aged person sitting in the chimney-corner, addressed himself unto him with admiration of his age till his mistake was rectified: for, "Oh, sir," said the young-old man, "I am not he whom you seek for, but his son; my father is farther off in the field." The same error is daily committed by the Romish Church, adoring the reverend brow and gray hairs of some ancient ceremonies, perchance but of some seven or eight hundred years' standing in the church, and mistake these for their fathers, of far greater age in the primitive times.

He desires to imitate the ancient fathers, as well in their piety as in their postures; not only conforming his hands and knees, but chiefly his heart, to their pattern. O the holiness of their living, and painfulness of their preaching! How full were they of mortified thoughts and heavenly meditations! Let us not make the ceremonial part of their lives only canonical, and the moral part thereof altogether apocrypha, imitating their devotion not in the fineness of the stuff, but only in the fashion of the making.

He carefully marks the declination of the Church from the primitive purity; observing how sometimes humble devotion was contented to lie down, whilst proud superstition got on her back. Yea, not only Frederick the Emperor, but many a godly father some hundreds of years before, held the pope's stirrup, and by their well-meaning simplicity gave occasion to his future greatness. He takes notice how their rhetorical hyperboles were afterwards accounted the just measure of dogmatical truths; how plain people took them at their word in their funeral apostrophes to the dead; how praying for the departed brought the fuel, under which after-ages kindled the fire of purgatory; how one ceremony begat another, there being no bounds in will-worship, wherewith one may sooner be wearied than satisfied, the inventors of new ceremonies endeavoring to supply in number what their conceits want in solidity; how men's souls, being in the full speed and career of the historical use of pictures, could not stop short, but must lash out into superstition; how the fathers, veiling their bonnets to Rome in civil courtesy, when making honorable mention thereof, are interpreted by modern papists to have done it in adoration of the idol of the pope's infallibility. All these things he ponders in his heart, observing both the times and places when and where they happened.

He is not zealous for the introducing of old, useless ceremonies. The mischief is, some that are most violent to bring such in, are most negligent to preach the cautions in using them; and simple people, like children in eating of fish, swallow bones and all, to their danger of choking. Besides, what is observed of horsehairs, that lying nine days in water they turn to snakes, so some ceremonies, though dead at first, in continuance of time quicken, get stings, and may do much mischief, especially if in such an age wherein the meddling of some have justly awaked the jealousy of all. When many popish tricks are abroad in the country, if then men meet with a ceremony which is a stranger, especially if it can give but a bad account of itself, no wonder if the watch take it up for one on suspicion.

He is not peremptory but conjectural in doubtful matters; not forcing others to his own opinion, but leaving them to their own liberty; not filling up all with his own conjectures, to leave no room for other men; nor tramples he on their credits, if in them he finds slips and mistakes. For here our souls have but one eye (the apostle saith, "we know in part"): be not proud if that chance to come athwart thy seeing side, which meets with the blind side of another.

He thankfully acknowledgeth those by whom he hath profited. Base-natured they who, when they have quenched their own thirst, stop up, at least muddy, the fountain. But our antiquary, if he be not the first founder of a commendable conceit, contents himself to be a benefactor to it in clearing and adorning it.

He affects not fanciful singularity in his behavior; nor cares to have a proper mark in writing of words, to disguise some peculiar letter from the ordinary character. Others, for fear travellers should take no notice that skill in antiquity dwells in such a head, hang out an antique hat for the sign, or use some obsolete garb in their garments, gestures, or discourse.

He doth not so adore the ancients as to despise the moderns. Grant them but dwarfs, yet stand they on giants' shoulders, and may see the further. Sure, as stout champions of truth follow in the rear as ever marched in the front. Besides, as one excellently observes, *Antiquitas seculi juventus mundi.** These times are the ancient times, when the world is ancient; and not those which we count ancient *ordine retrogrado*, by a computation backwards from ourselves.

THE GOOD PARISHIONER.

WE will only describe his church-reference; his civil part hath and shall be met with under other heads. Conceive him to live under such a faithful minister as before was charactered, as, either judging charitably that all pastors are such, or wishing heartily that they were.

Though near to the church, he is not far from God. Like unto Justus, Acts xviii. 8, "one that worshipped God, and his house joined hard to the synagogue." Otherwise, if his distance from the church be great, his diligence is the greater to come thither in season.

He is timely at the beginning of prayer. Yet, as Tully charged some dissolute people for being such sluggards that they never saw the

* Sir Francis Bacon, *Advancement of Learning.*

sun rising or setting, as being always up after the one, and abed before the other; so some negligent people never hear prayers begun, or sermon ended, the confession being past before they come, and the blessing not come before they are passed away.

In sermon he sets himself to hear God in the minister. Therefore divesteth he himself of all prejudice, the jaundice in the eyes of the soul, presenting colors false unto it. He hearkens very attentively: 't is a shame when the church itself is *cœmeterium*, wherein the living sleep above ground as the dead do beneath.

At every point that concerns himself, he turns down a leaf in his heart; and rejoiceth that God's word hath pierced him, as hoping that whilst his soul smarts, it heals. And as it is no manners for him that hath good venison before him to ask whence it came, but rather fairly to fall to it, so, hearing an excellent sermon, he never inquires whence the preacher had it, or whether it was not before in print, but falls aboard to practise it.

He accuseth not his minister of spite for particularizing him. It does not follow that the archer aimed because the arrow hit. Rather our parishioner reasoneth thus: If my sin be notorious, how could the minister miss it? if secret, how could he hit it without God's direction? But foolish hearers make even the bells of Aaron's garments to clink as they think. And a guilty conscience is like a whirlpool, drawing in all to itself which otherwise would pass by. One, causelessly disaffected to his minister, complained that he in his last sermon had personally inveighed against him, and accused him thereof to a grave religious gentleman in the parish. "Truly," said the gentleman, "I had thought in his sermon he had meant me, for it touched my heart." This rebated the edge of the other's anger.

His tithes he pays willingly with cheerfulness. How many part with God's portions grudgingly, or else pinch it in the paying. *Decimum*, the tenth, amongst the Romans was ever taken for what was best or biggest. It falls out otherwise in paying of tithes, where the least and leanest are shifted off to make that number.

He hides not himself from any parish office which seeks for him. If chosen churchwarden, he is not busily idle, rather to trouble than reform, presenting all things but those which he should. If overseer of the poor, he is careful the rates be made indifferent (whose inequality oftentimes is more burdensome than the sum) and well disposed of. He measures not people's wants by their clamorous complaining, and dispenseth more to those that deserve than to them that only need relief.

He is bountiful in contributing to the repair of God's house. For though he be not of their opinion who would have the churches under the gospel conformed to the magnificence of Solomon's Temple, (whose porch would serve us for a church,) and adorn them so gaudily that devotion is more distracted than raised, and men's souls rather dazzled than lightened, yet he conceives it fitting that such sacred places should be handsomely and decently maintained: the rather, because the climacterical year of many churches from their first foundation may seem to happen in our days; so old, that their ruin is threatened if not speedily repaired.

He is respectful to his minister's widow and posterity, for his sake. When the only daughter of Peter Martyr was, through the riot and prodigality of her husband, brought to extreme poverty, the State of Zurich, out of grateful remembrance of her father, supported her with bountiful maintenance. My prayers shall be, that ministers' widows and children may never stand in need of such relief, and may never want such relief when they stand in need.

THE GOOD SCHOOLMASTER

THERE is scarce any profession in the commonwealth more necessary, which is so slightly performed. The reasons whereof I conceive to be these: First, young scholars make this calling their refuge, yea, perchance before they have taken any degree in the university, commence schoolmasters in the country, as if nothing else were required to set up this profession but only a rod and a ferula. Secondly, others, who are able, use it only as a passage to better preferment, to patch the rents in their present fortune till they can provide a new one, and betake themselves to some more gainful calling. Thirdly, they are disheartened from doing their best with the miserable reward which in some places they receive, being masters to the children and slaves to their parents. Fourthly, being grown rich, they grow negligent, and scorn to touch the school but by the proxy of an usher. But see how well our schoolmaster behaves himself.

His genius inclines him with delight to his profession. Some men had as lief be schoolboys as schoolmasters, to be tied to the school, as Cooper's "Dictionary" and Scapula's "Lexicon" are chained to the desk therein; and though great scholars, and skilful in other arts, are bunglers in this: but God of his goodness hath fitted several men for several callings, that the necessity of Church and State in all conditions may be provided for. So that he who beholds the fabric thereof may say, "God hewed out this stone, and appointed it to lie in this very place, for it would fit none other so well, and here it doth most excellent." And thus God mouldeth some for a schoolmaster's life, undertaking it with desire and delight, and discharging it with dexterity and happy success.

He studieth his scholars' natures as carefully as they their books; and ranks their dispositions into several forms. And though it may seem difficult for him in a great school to descend to all particulars, yet experienced schoolmasters may quickly make a grammar of boys' natures, and reduce them all, saving some few exceptions, to these general rules.

1. Those that are ingenious and industrious. The conjunction of two such planets in a youth presage much good unto him. To such a lad a frown may be a whipping, and a whipping a death; yea, where their master whips them once, shame whips them all the week after. Such natures he useth with all gentleness.

2. Those that are ingenious and idle. These think, with the hare in the fable, that running with snails (so they count the rest of their

school-fellows) they shall come soon enough to the post, though sleeping a good while before their starting. Oh, a good rod would finely take them napping.

3. Those that are dull and diligent. Wines, the stronger they be, the more lees they have when they are new. Many boys are muddy-headed till they be clarified with age, and such afterwards prove the best. Bristol diamonds are both bright and squared and pointed by nature, and yet are soft and worthless; whereas, Orient ones in India are rough and rugged naturally. Hard, rugged, and dull natures of youth acquit themselves afterwards the jewels of the country, and therefore their dulness at first is to be borne with, if they be diligent. That schoolmaster deserves to be beaten himself who beats nature in a boy for a fault. And I question whether all the whipping in the world can make their parts, which are naturally sluggish, rise one minute before the hour nature hath appointed.

4. Those that are invincibly dull, and negligent also. Correction may reform the latter, not amend the former. All the whetting in the world can never set a razor's edge on that which hath no steel in it. Such boys he consigneth over to other professions. Shipwrights and boatmakers will choose those crooked pieces of timber which other carpenters refuse. Those

may make excellent merchants and mechanics which will not serve for scholars.

He is able, diligent, and methodical in his teaching; not leading them rather in a circle than forwards. He minces his precepts for children to swallow, hanging clogs on the nimbleness of his own soul, that his scholars may go along with him.

He is, and will be known to be, an absolute monarch in his school. If cockering mothers proffer him money to purchase their sons an exemption from his rod, (to live as it were in a peculiar, out of their master's jurisdiction,) with disdain he refuseth it, and scorns the late custom in some places of commuting whipping into money, and ransoming boys from the rod at a set price. If he hath a stubborn youth, correction-proof, he debaseth not his authority by contesting with him, but fairly, if he can, puts him away before his obstinacy hath infected others.

He is moderate in inflicting deserved correction. Many a schoolmaster better answereth the name παιδοτρίβης than παιδαγωγός, rather tearing his scholars' flesh with whipping than giving them good education. No wonder if his scholars hate the Muses, being presented unto them in the shapes of fiends and furies. Junius complains *de insolenti carnificina* of his schoolmaster, by whom *conscindebatur flagris septies aut octies in dies singulos.* Yea, hear the lamentable verses of poor Tusser in his own life: —

"From Paul's I went, to Eton sent,
To learn straightways the Latin phrase,
Where fifty-three stripes given to me
At once I had.

"For fault but small, or none at all,
It came to pass thus beat I was;
See Udal,* see the mercy of thee
To me poor lad."

Such an Orbilius mars more scholars than he makes: their tyranny hath caused many tongues to stammer, which spake plain by nature, and whose stuttering at first was nothing else but fears quavering on their speech at their master's presence; and whose mauling them about their heads hath dulled those who, in quickness, exceeded their master.

He makes his school free to him who sues to him *in forma pauperis.* And surely learning is the greatest alms that can be given. But he is a beast who, because the poor scholar cannot pay him his wages, pays the scholar in his whipping. Rather are diligent lads to be encouraged with all excitements to learning. This minds me of what I have heard concerning Mr. Bust, that worthy late schoolmaster of Eton, who would never suffer any wandering

* Nich. Udal, schoolmaster of Eton, in the reign of King Henry the Eighth.

begging scholar (such as justly the statute hath ranked in the forefront of rogues) to come into his school, but would thrust him out with earnestness, (however privately charitable unto him,) lest his schoolboys should be disheartened from their books by seeing some scholars, after their studying in the university, preferred to beggary.

He spoils not a good school to make thereof a bad college, therein to teach his scholars logic. For, besides that logic may have an action of trespass against grammar for encroaching on her liberties, syllogisms are solecisms taught in the school, and oftentimes they are forced afterwards in the university to unlearn the fumbling skill they had before.

Out of his school he is no whit pedantical in carriage or discourse ; contenting himself to be rich in Latin, though he doth not jingle with it in every company wherein he comes.

To conclude, let this amongst other motives make schoolmasters careful in their place, that the eminencies of their scholars have commended the memories of their schoolmasters to posterity, who otherwise in obscurity had altogether been forgotten. Who had ever heard of R. Bond, in Lancashire, but for the breeding of learned Ascham, his scholar? or of Hartgrave, in Brundly school, in the same county, but because he was the first did teach worthy

Doctor Whitaker? Nor do I honor the memory of Mulcaster for anything so much as for his scholar, that gulf of learning, Bishop Andrews. This made the Athenians, the day before the great feast of Theseus, their founder, to sacrifice a ram to the memory of Conidas, his schoolmaster that first instructed him.

THE GENERAL ARTIST.

I KNOW the general cavil against general learning is this, that *aliquis in omnibus est nullus in singulis;* he that sips of many arts drinks of none. However, we must know that all learning, which is but one grand science, hath so homogeneal a body, that the parts thereof do with a mutual service relate to, and communicate strength and lustre each to other. Our artist, knowing language to be the key of learning, thus begins.

His tongue, being but one by nature, he gets cloven by art and industry. Before the confusion of Babel, all the world was one continent in language; since divided into several tongues, as several islands. Grammar is the ship, by benefit whereof we pass from one to another, in the learned languages generally spoken in no country. His mother tongue was like the dull music of a monochord, which, by study, he turns into the harmony of several instruments.

He first gaineth skill in the Latin and Greek tongues. On the credit of the former alone he may trade in discourse over all Christendom: but the Greek, though not so generally spoken, is known with no less profit and more pleasure. The joints of her compounded words are so naturally oiled, that they run nimbly on the tongue; which makes them, though long, never tedious, because significant. Besides, it is full and stately in sound: only it pities our artist to see the vowels therein racked in pronouncing them, hanging oftentimes one way by their native force, and haled another by their accents which countermand them.

Hence he proceeds to the Hebrew, the mother tongue of the world. More pains than quickness of wit is required to get it, and with daily exercise he continues it. Apostacy herein is usual to fall totally from the language by a little neglect. As for the Arabic, and other Oriental languages, he rather makes sallies and incursions into them than any solemn sitting before them.

Then he applies his study to logic and ethics. The latter makes a man's soul mannerly and wise; but as for logic, that is the armory of reason, furnished with all offensive and defensive weapons. There are syllogisms, long swords; enthymemes, short daggers; dilemmas, two-edged swords that cut on both sides; sorites, chain-shot: and for the defensive, distinctions, which are shields; retortions, which are targets with a pike in the midst of them, both to defend and oppose. From hence he raiseth his studies to the knowledge of physics, the great hall of nature, and metaphysics, the closet thereof; and is careful not to wade therein so far, till, by subtile distinguishing of notions, he confounds himself.

He is skilful in rhetoric, which gives a speech color, as logic doth favor, and both together beauty. Though some condemn rhetoric as the mother of lies, speaking more than the truth in hyperboles, less in her miosis, otherwise in her metaphors, contrary in her ironies, yet is there excellent use of all these when disposed of with judgment. Nor is he a stranger to poetry, which is music in words; nor to music, which is poetry in sound; both excellent sauce, but they have lived and died poor that made them their meat.

Mathematics he moderately studieth to his great contentment; using it as ballast for his soul, yet to fix it, not to stall it; nor suffers he it to be so unmannerly as to jostle out other arts. As for judicial astrology (which hath the least judgment in it), this vagrant hath been whipped out of all learned corporations. If our artist lodgeth her in the out-rooms of his soul for a night or two, it is rather to hear than believe her relations.

Hence he makes his progress into the study of history. Nestor, who lived three ages, was accounted the wisest man in the world. But the historian may make himself wise by living as many ages as have passed since the beginning of the world. His books enable him to maintain discourse, who, besides the stock of his own experience, may spend on the common purse of his reading. This directs him in his life, so that he makes the shipwrecks of others sea-marks to himself; yea, accidents which others start from for their strangeness, he welcomes as his wonted acquaintance, having found precedents for them formerly. Without history a man's soul is purblind, seeing only the things which almost touch his eyes.

He is well seen in chronology, without which history is but a heap of tales. If by the laws of the land he is counted a natural who hath not wit enough to tell twenty, or to tell his age, he shall not pass with me for wise in learning who cannot tell the age of the world, and count hundreds of years; I mean, not so critically as to solve all doubts arising thence, but that he may be able to give some tolerable account thereof. He is also acquainted with cosmography, treating of the world in whole joints; with chorography, shredding it into countries; and with topography, mincing it into particular places.

Thus, taking these sciences in their general latitude, he hath finished the round circle or golden ring of the arts; only he keeps a place for the diamond to be set in: I mean for that predominant profession of law, physic, divinity, or state policy, which he intends for his principal calling hereafter.

THE GOOD MERCHANT

IS one who, by his trading, claspeth the islands to the continent, and one country to another; an excellent gardener, who makes England bear wine, and oil, and spices; yea, herein goes beyond nature in causing that *omnis fert omnia tellus.* He wrongs neither himself, nor the commonwealth, nor private chapmen which buy commodities of him. As for his behavior towards the commonwealth, it far surpasses my skill to give any rules thereof: only this I know, that to export things of necessity, and to bring in foreign needless toys, makes a rich merchant, and a poor kingdom; for the State loseth her radical moisture, and gets little better than sweat in exchange, except the necessaries which are exported be exceeding plentiful,—which then, though necessary in their own nature, become superfluous through their abundance. We will content ourselves to give some general advertisements concerning his behavior towards his chapmen; whom he useth well in the quantity, quality, and price of the commodities he sells them.

He wrongs not the buyer in number, weight, or measure. These are the landmarks of all trading, which must not be removed; for such cozenage were worse than open felony. First, because they rob a man of his purse, and never bid him stand. Secondly, because highway thieves defy, but these pretend justice. Thirdly, as much as lies in their power, they endeavor to make God accessary to their cozenage, deceiving by pretending his weights. For God is the principal clerk of the market: "all the weights of the bag are his work." *Prov.* xvi. 11.

He never warrants any ware for good but what is so indeed. Otherwise he is a thief, and may be a murderer, if selling such things as are applied inwardly. Besides, in such a case, he counts himself guilty if he selleth such wares as are bad, though without his knowledge, if avouching them for good; because he may, professeth, and is bound to be master in his own mystery, and therefore in conscience must recompense the buyer's loss, except he gives him an item to buy it at his own adventure.

He either tells the faults in his ware, or abates proportionably in the price he demands; for then the low value shows the viciousness of it. Yet, commonly, when merchants depart with their commodities, we hear (as in funeral orations) all the virtues but none of the faults thereof.

He never demands out of distance of the price he intends to take: if not always within the touch, yet within the reach of what he means to sell for. Now, we must know there be four several prices of vendible things. First, the price of the market, which ebbs and flows according to the plenty or scarcity of coin, commodities, and chapmen. Secondly, the price of friendship, which perchance is more giving than selling, and therefore not so proper at this time. Thirdly, the price of fancy, as twenty pounds or more for a dog or hawk, when no such inherent worth can naturally be in them, but by the buyer's and seller's fancy reflecting on them. Yet I believe the money may be lawfully taken. First, because the seller sometimes on those terms is as loath to forego it as the buyer is willing to have it; and I know no standard herein whereby men's affections may be measured. Secondly, it being a matter of pleasure, and men able and willing, let them pay for it: *volenti non fit injuria.* Lastly, there is the price of cozenage, which our merchant from his heart detests and abhors.

He makes not advantage of his chapman's ignorance, chiefly if referring himself to his honesty; where the seller's conscience is all the buyer's skill, who makes him both seller and judge, so that he doth not so much ask as order what he must pay. When one told old Bishop Latimer that the cutler had cozened him in making him pay twopence for a knife not (in those days) worth a penny, — "No," quoth Latimer, "he cozened not me, but his own conscience." On the other side, St. Augustine tells us of a seller who out of ignorance asked for a book far less than it was worth, and the buyer (conceive himself to be the man if you please) of his own accord gave him the full value thereof.

He makes not the buyer pay the shot for his prodigality; as when the merchant, through his own ignorance or ill husbandry, hath bought dear, he will not bring in his unnecessary expenses on the buyer's score; and in such a case he is bound to sell cheaper than he bought.

Selling by retail, he may justify the taking of greater gain; because of his care, pains, and cost of fetching those wares from the fountain, and in parcelling and dividing them. Yet, because retailers trade commonly with those who have least skill what they buy, and commonly sell to the poorer sort of people, they must be careful not to grate on their necessity.

But how long shall I be retailing out rules to this merchant? It would employ a casuist an apprenticeship of years: take our Saviour's wholesale rule, "Whatsoever ye would have men do unto you, do you unto them; for this is the Law and the Prophets."

THE GOOD YEOMAN.

IS a gentleman in ore, whom the next age may see refined; and is the wax capable of a gentle impression, when the prince shall stamp it. Wise Solon (who accounted Tellus the Athenian the most happy man for living privately on his own lands) would surely have pronounced the English yeomanry a fortunate condition, living in the temperate zone, betwixt greatness and want,—an estate of people almost peculiar to England. France and Italy are like a die which hath no points between cinq and ace, nobility and peasantry. Their walls, though high, must needs be hollow, wanting filling-stones. Indeed, Germany hath her boors, like our yeomen, but, by a tyrannical appropriation of nobility to some few ancient families, their yeomen are excluded from ever rising higher to clarify their bloods. In England the temple of honor is bolted against none who have passed through the temple of virtue; nor is a capacity to be gentle denied to our yeoman who thus behaves himself.

He wears russet clothes, but makes golden payment, having tin in his buttons, and silver in his pocket. If he chance to appear in clothes above his rank, it is to grace some great man with his service, and then he blusheth at his own bravery. Otherwise, he is the surest landmark, whence foreigners may take aim of the ancient English customs; the gentry more floating after foreign fashions.

In his house he is bountiful both to strangers and poor people. Some hold, when hospitality died in England, she gave her last groan amongst the yeomen of Kent. And still at our yeoman's table you shall have as many joints as dishes: no meat disguised with strange sauces; no straggling joint of a sheep in the midst of a pasture of grass, beset with sallads on every side; but solid substantial food: no servitors (more nimble with their hands than the guests with their teeth) take away meat before stomachs are taken away. Here you have that which in itself is good, made better by the store of it, and best by the welcome to it.

He hath a great stroke in making a knight of the shire. Good reason; for he makes a whole line in the subsidy book, where whatsoever he is rated he pays, without any regret, not caring how much his purse is let blood, so it be done by the advice of the physicians of the state.

He seldom goes far abroad, and his credit stretcheth further than his travel. He goes not to London, but *se defendendo*, to save himself of a fine, being returned of a jury, where, seeing the king once, he prays for him ever afterwards.

In his own country he is a main man in juries, where, if the judge please to open his eyes in matter of law, he needs not be led by the nose in matters of fact. He is very observant of the judge's "item," when it follows the truth's *imprimis;* otherwise, (though not mutinous in a jury,) he cares not whom he displeaseth, so he pleaseth his own conscience.

He improveth his land to a double value by his good husbandry. Some grounds that wept with water, or frowned with thorns, by draining the one and clearing the other, he makes both to laugh and sing with corn. By marl and limestones burnt, he bettereth his ground, and his industry worketh miracles by turning stones into bread. Conquest and good husbandry both enlarge the king's dominions: the one by the sword, making the acres more in number; the other by the plough, making the same acres more in value. Solomon saith, "The king himself is maintained by husbandry." Pythis, a king, having discovered rich mines in his kingdom, employed all his people in digging of them, whence tilling was wholly neglected, insomuch as a great famine ensued. His queen, sensible of the calamities of the country, invited the king her husband to dinner, as he came home hungry from overseeing his workmen in the mines. She so contrived it that the bread and meat were most artificially made of gold; and the king was much delighted with the conceit thereof, till at last he called for real meat to satisfy his hunger. "Nay," said the queen, "if you employ all your subjects in your mines, you must expect to feed upon gold; for nothing else can your kingdom afford."

In time of famine, he is the Joseph of the country, and keeps the poor from starving. Then he tameth his stacks of corn, which not his covetousness but providence hath reserved for time of need, and to his poor neighbors abateth somewhat of the high price of the market. The neighbor gentry court him for his acquaintance, which either he modestly waveth, or thankfully accepteth, but no way greedily desireth. He insults not on the ruins of a decayed gentleman, but pities and relieves him; and as he is called "good man," he desires to answer to the name, and to be so indeed.

In war, though he serveth on foot, he is ever mounted on a high spirit; as being a slave to none, and a subject only to his own prince. Innocence and independence make a brave spirit: whereas otherwise one must ask his leave to be valiant on whom he depends. Therefore, if a state run up all to noblemen and gentlemen, so that the husbandmen be only mere laborers, or cottagers, (which one calls but housed beggars,) it may have good cavalry, but never good bands of foot; so that their armies will be like those birds called *apodes*, without feet, always only flying on their wings of horse. Wherefore, to make good infantry, it requireth men bred, not in a servile or indigent fashion, but in some free and plentiful manner. Wisely, therefore, did that knowing prince, King Henry the Seventh, provide laws for the increase of his yeomanry, that his kingdom should not be like to coppice-woods, where, the staddles being left too thick, all runs to bushes and briers, and there is little clean underwood. For, enacting that houses used to husbandry should be kept up with a competent proportion of land, he did secretly sow hydra's teeth, whereupon (according to the poet's fiction) should rise up armed men for the service of this kingdom.

THE HANDICRAFTSMAN.

HE is a necessary member in a commonwealth; for though nature, which hath armed most other creatures, sent man naked into the world, yet in giving him hands and wit to use them, in effect she gave him shells, scales, paws, claws, horns, tusks, with all offensive and defensive weapons of beasts, fish, and fowl, which, by the help of his hands, in imitation he may provide for himself; and herein the skill of our artisan doth consist.

His trade is such whereby he provides things necessary for mankind. What St. Paul saith of the natural, is also true of the politic body: those members of the body are much more necessary which seem most feeble. Mean trades for profit are most necessary in the State, and a house may better want a gallery than a kitchen. The Philistines knew this when they massacred all the smiths in Israel, who might worse be spared than all the usurers therein, and whose hammers nail the commonwealth together, being necessary both in peace and war.

Or else his trade contributeth to man's lawful pleasure. God is not so hard a master but that he alloweth his servants sauce (besides hunger) to eat with their meat.

But in no case will he be of such a trade which is a mere pander to man's lust, and only serves their wantonness (which is pleasure run stark mad) and foolish curiosity. Yet are there too many extant of such professions, which, one would think, should stand in daily fear lest the world should turn wise, and so all their trades be cashiered, but that (be it spoken to their shame) 't is as safe a tenure to hold a livelihood by men's riot as by their necessity.

The wares he makes show good to the eye, but prove better in the use. For he knows if he sets his mark (the Tower-stamp of his credit) on any bad wares, he sets a deeper brand on his own conscience. Nothing hath more debased the credit of our English cloth beyond the seas than the deceitfulness in making them, since the fox hath crept under the fleece of the sheep.

By his ingeniousness he leaves his art better than he found it. Herein the Hollanders are excellent, where children get their living, when but newly they have gotten their life, by their industry. Indeed, nature may seem to have made those Netherlanders the younger brethren of mankind, allowing them little land, and that also standing in daily fear of a deluge of the sea: but such is their painfulness and ingenuity, hating laziness as much as they love liberty, that what commodities grow not on their country by nature, they graft on it by art, and have wonderfully improved all making of manufactures, stuffs, clocks, watches. These latter at first were made so great and heavy, it was rather a burden than an ornament to wear them; though since, watches have been made as light and little as many that wear them make of their time.

He is willing to communicate his skill to posterity. An invention, though found, is lost if not imparted. But as it is reported of some old toads, that before their death they suck up the jelly in their own heads (which otherwise would be hardened into a precious stone) out of spite, that men should receive no benefit thereby, so some envious artisans will have their cunning die with them, that none may be the better for it, and had rather all mankind should lose than any man gain by them.

He seldom attaineth to any very great estate: except his trade hath some outlets and excursions into wholesale and merchandise; otherwise mere artificers cannot heap up much wealth. It is difficult for gleaners, without stealing whole sheaves, to fill a barn. His chief wealth consisteth in enough, and that he can live comfortably, and leave his children the inheritance of their education.

Yet he is a grand benefactor to the commonwealth. England, in former ages, like a dainty dame, partly out of state, but more out of laziness, would not suckle the fruit of her own body, to make the best to battle and improve her own commodities, but put them out to nurse to the Netherlanders, who were well paid for their pains. In those days, the sword and the plough so took up all men's employments that clothing was wholly neglected, and scarce any other webs to be found in houses than what the spiders did make. But since, she hath seen and mended her error, making the best use of her own wool; and indeed the riches of a kingdom doth consist in driving the home commodities thereof as far as they will go, working them to their very perfection, employing more handicrafts thereby. The sheep feeds more with his fleece than his flesh, doing the one but once, but the other once a year, many families subsisting by the working thereof.

We have cause to hope, that, as we have seen the cities Dornicks and Arras brought over into England, so posterity may see all Flanders brought hither; I mean that their works shall be here imitated, and that either our land shall be taught to bear foreign commodities, or our people taught to forbear the using of them.

I should now come to give the description of the day-laborer, (of whom we have only a dearth in a plentiful harvest,) but seeing his character is so coincident with the hired servant, it may well be spared. And now we will rise from the hand to the arm, and come to describe the soldier.

THE GOOD SOLDIER.

A SOLDIER is one of a lawful, necessary, commendable, and honorable profession; yea, God himself may seem to be one free of the company of soldiers, in that he styleth himself "a man of war." Now, though many hate soldiers as the twigs of the rod war, wherewith God scourgeth wanton countries into repentance, yet is their calling so needful, that were not some soldiers we must be all soldiers, daily employed to defend our own, the world would grow so licentious.

He keepeth a clear and quiet conscience in his breast, which otherwise will gnaw out the roots of all valor; for vicious soldiers are compassed with enemies on all sides, their foes without them, and an ambush within them of fleshly lusts, which, as St. Peter saith, "fight against the soul." None fitter to go to war than those who have made their peace with God in Christ; for such a man's soul is an impregnable fort: it cannot be scaled with ladders, for it reacheth up to heaven; nor be broken by batteries, for it is walled with brass; nor undermined by pioneers, for he is founded on a rock; nor betrayed by treason, for faith itself keeps it; nor be burnt by grenadoes, for he can quench the fiery darts of the devil; nor be forced by famine, for a good conscience is a continual feast.

He chiefly avoids those sins to which soldiers are taxed as most subject: namely, common swearing, which impaireth one's credit by degrees, and maketh all his promises not to be trusted; for he who for no profit will sin against God, for small profit will trespass against his neighbor; and drinking. When valiant Zisca, near Pilsen, in Bohemia, fought against his enemies, he commanded the women which followed his army to cast their kerchiefs and partlets on the ground, wherein their enemies, being entangled by their spurs, (for, though horsemen, they were forced to alight and fight on foot, through the roughness of the place,) were slain before they could unloose their feet. A deep moral may be gathered hence; and women have often been the nets to catch and ensnare the souls of many martial men.

He counts his prince's lawful command to be his sufficient warrant to fight. In a defensive war, when his country is hostilely invaded, 't is pity but his neck should hang in suspense with his conscience that doubts to fight; in offensive war, though the case be harder, the common soldier is not to dispute, but do his prince's command. Otherwise princes, before they levy an army of soldiers, must first levy an army of casuists and confessors to satisfy each scrupulous soldier in point of right to the war; and the most cowardly will be the most conscientious to multiply doubts eternally. Besides, causes of war are so complicated and perplexed, so many things falling in the prosecution as may alter the original state thereof; and private soldiers have neither calling nor ability to dive into such mysteries. But if the conscience of a counsellor or commander-in-chief remonstrates in himself the unlawfulness of this war, he is bound humbly to represent to his prince his reasons against it.

He esteemeth all hardship easy through hopes of victory. Moneys are the sinews of war; yet if these sinews should chance to be shrunk, and pay casually fall short, he takes a fit of this convulsion patiently. He is contented, though in cold weather his hands must be their own fire, and warm themselves with working; though he be better armed against their enemies than the weather, and his corselet wholler than his clothes; though he hath more fasts and vigils in his almanac than the Romish Church did ever enjoin: he patiently endureth drought for desire of honor, and one thirst quencheth another. In a word, though much indebted to his own back and belly, and unable to pay them, yet he hath credit himself, and confidently runs on ticket with himself, hoping the next victory will discharge all scores with advantage.

He looks at and also through his wages, at God's glory, and his country's good. He counts his pay an honorable addition, but no valuable compensation for his pains; for what proportion is there betwixt four shillings a week and adventuring his life? I cannot see how their calling can be lawful, who, for greater wages, will fight on any side against their own king and cause; yea, as false witnesses were hired against our blessed Saviour, (money will make the mouths of men plead against their Maker,) so were the giants now in the world, who, as the poets feigned, made war against God himself, and should they offer great pay, they would not want mercenary soldiers to assist them.

He attends with all readiness on the commands of his general; rendering up his own judgment in obedience to the will and pleasure of his leader, and by an implicit faith believing all is best which he enjoineth; lest otherwise he be served as the French soldier was in Scotland, some eighty years since, who first mounted the bulwark of a fort besieged, whereupon ensued the gaining of the fort: but Marescal de Thermes, the French general, first knighted him, and then hanged him within an hour after, because he had done it without commandment.

He will not in a bravery expose himself to needless peril. 'T is madness to halloo in the ears of sleeping temptation, to awaken it against one's self, or to go out of his calling to find a danger: but if a danger meets him (as he walks in his vocation), he neither stands still, starts aside, nor steps backward, but either goes over it with valor, or under it with patience. All single duels he detesteth, as having, first, no command in God's word; yea, this arbitrary deciding causes by the sword subverts the fundamental laws of the Scripture: secondly, no example in God's word, that of David and Goliath moving in an higher sphere, as extraordinary: thirdly, it tempts God to work a miracle for man's pleasure, and to invert the course of nature, whereby otherwise the stronger will beat the weaker: fourthly, each dueller challengeth his king as unable or unwilling legally to right him, and therefore he usurps the office himself: fifthly, if slaying, he hazards his neck to the halter; if slain, in heat of malice, without repentance, he adventures his soul to the devil.

Object. But there are some intricate cases (as in titles of land), which cannot otherwise be decided. Seeing, therefore, that in such difficulties the right in question cannot be delivered by any judicial proceedings, then it must be determined by the sword.

Answ. Such a right may better be lost than to light a candle from hell to find it out, if the judges cannot find a middle way to part it betwixt them. Besides, in such a case, duels are no *medium proportionatum* to find out the truth, as never appointed by God to that purpose. Nor doth it follow that he hath the best in right who hath the best in fight; for he that reads the lawfulness of actions by their events holds the wrong end of the book upwards.

Object. But suppose an army of thirty thousand infidels ready to fight against ten thousand Christians, yet so that at last the infidels are contented to try the day upon the valor of a single champion; whether in such a case may not a Christian undertake to combat with him, the rather because the treble odds before is thereby reduced to terms of equality, and so the victory is made more probable.

Answ. The victory was more probable before; because it is more likely God will bless his own means, than means of man's appointing; and it is his prerogative to give victory, as well by few as by many. Probability of conquest is not to be measured by the eye of human reason, contrary to the square of God's word. Besides, I question whether it be lawful for a Christian army to derive their right of fighting God's battles to any single man. For the title every man hath to promote God's glory is so invested and inherent in his own particular person, that he cannot pass it over to another. None may appear in God's service by an attorney; and when religion is at the stake, there must be no lookers-on (except impotent people, who also help by their prayers), and every one is bound to lay his shoulders to the work. Lastly, would to God no duels might be fought till this case came into question. But how many daily fall out upon a more false, slight, and flitting ground than the sands of Calais whereon they fight: especially, seeing there is an honorable court appointed, or some other equivalent way, for taking up such quarrels, and allowing reparations to the party injured.

Object. But reputation is so spiritual a thing, it is inestimable, and honor falls not under valuation: besides, to complain to the civil magistrate showeth no manhood, but is like a child's crying to his father, when he is only beaten by his equal; and my enemy's forced acknowledgment of his fault (enjoined him by the court) shows rather his submission to the laws than to me. But if I can civilize his rudeness by my sword, and chastise him into submission, then he sings his penitential song in the true tune, and it comes naturally indeed.

Answ. Honorable persons in that court are the most competent judges of honor; and though credit be as tender as the apple of the eye, yet such curious oculists can cure a blemish therein. And why, I pray, is it more disgrace to repair to the magistrate for redress in reputation than to have recourse to him in actions of trespass? The pretence of a forced submission is nothing, all submissions having *aliquid violentum* in them; and even the evangelical repentance of God's servants hath a mixture of legal terror frighting them thereto.

Object. But gownmen speak out of an antipathy they bear to fighting: should we be ruled by them, we must break all our swords into penknives; and lawyers, to enlarge their gains, send prohibitions to remove suits from the camps to their courts; divines are not to be consulted with herein, as ignorant of the principles of honor.

Answ. Indeed, honor is a word of course in the talk of roaring boys, and pure enough in itself, except their mouths soil it by often using of it: but indeed God is the fountain of honor, God's word the charter of honor, and godly men the best judges of it; nor is it any stain of cowardliness for one to fear hell and damnation.

We may therefore conclude that the laws of duelling, as the laws of drinking, had their original from the devil; and therefore the declining of needless quarrels in our soldier, no abatement of honor. I commend his discretion and valor, who, walking in London streets, met a gallant, who cried to him a pretty distance beforehand, "I will have the wall." "Yea," answered he, "and take the house too, if you can but agree with the landlord." But when God, and his prince, calls for him, our soldier

Had rather die ten times than once survive his credit. Though life be sweet, it shall not flatter the palate of his soul, as with the sweetness of life to make him swallow down the bitterness of an eternal disgrace. He begrudgeth not to get to his side a probability of victory by the certainty of his own death, and flieth from nothing so much as from the mention of flying. And though some say he is a madman, that will purchase honor so dearly with his blood as that he cannot live to enjoy what he hath bought, our soldier knows that he shall possess the reward of his valor with God in heaven, and also making the world his executor, leave to it the rich inheritance of his memory.

Yet in some cases he counts it no disgrace to yield, where it is impossible to conquer; as when swarms of enemies crowd about him, so that he shall rather be stifled than wounded to death: in such a case, if quarter be offered him, he may take it with more honor than the other can give it; and if he throws up his desperate game, he may happily win the next; whereas, if he playeth it out to the last, he shall certainly lose it and himself. But if he be to fall into the hand of a barbarous enemy, whose giving him quarter is but reprieving him for a more ignominious death, he had rather disburse his life at the present than to take day to fall into the hands of such remorseless creditors.

He makes none the object of his cruelty, which cannot be the object of his fear. Lions, they say, (except forced with hunger,) will not prey on women and children, though I would wish none to try the truth hereof: the truly valiant will not hurt women or infants, nor will they be cruel to old men. What conquest is it to strike him up, who stands but on one leg, and hath the other foot in the grave? But arrant cowards (such as would conquer victory itself, if it should stand in their way as they fly) count themselves never evenly matched except they have threefold odds on their side, and esteem their enemy never disarmed till they be dead. Such love to show a nature steeped in gall of passion, and display the ignoble tyranny of prevailing dastards: these being thus valiant against no resistance, will make no resistance when they meet with true valor.

He counts it murder to kill any in cold blood. Indeed, in taking cities by assault (especially when soldiers have suffered long in a hard siege), it is pardonable what present passion doth with a sudden thrust; but a premeditated back-blow in cold blood is base. Some excuse there is for blood enraged, and no wonder if that scaldeth which boileth; but when men shall call a consultation in their soul, and issue thence a deliberate act, the more advised the deed is, the less advised it is, when men raise their own passions, and are not raised by them; especially if fair quarter be first granted; an alms which he who gives to-day may crave to-morrow; yea, he that hath the hilt in his hand in the morning may have the point at his throat ere night.

He doth not barbarously abuse the bodies of his dead enemies. We find that Hercules was the first (the most valiant are ever the most merciful) that ever suffered his enemies to carry away their dead bodies after they had been put to the sword. Belike, before his time they cruelly cut the corpses in pieces, or cast them to the wild beasts.

In time of plenty he provides for want hereafter. Yet, generally, soldiers (as if they counted one treasurer in an army were enough) so hate covetousness that they cannot affect providence for the future, and come home with more marks in their bodies than pence in their pockets.

He is willing and joyful to embrace peace on good conditions. The procreation of peace, and not the satisfying of men's lusts and liberties, is the end of war. Yet how many, having war for their possession, desire a perpetuity thereof! Wiser men than King Henry the Eighth's fool, use to cry in fair weather, whose harvest being only in storms, they themselves desire to raise them; wherefore fearing peace will starve whom war hath fatted, and to render themselves the more useful, they prolong discord to the utmost, and could wish when swords are once drawn that all scabbards might be cut asunder.

He is as quiet and painful in peace as courageous in war. If he hath not gotten already enough whereon comfortably to subsist, he rebetakes himself to his former calling he had before the war began: the wielding of his sword hath not made him unwieldy to do any other work, and put his bones out of joint to take pains. Hence comes it to pass that some take by-courses on the highways, and death, whom they honorably fought for in the field, meets them in a worse place.

But we leave our soldier, seeking by his virtues to ascend from a private place, by the degrees of sergeant, lieutenant, captain, colonel, till he come to be a general, and then, God willing, you shall have his example.

THE GOOD GENERAL.

THE soldier, whom we formerly described, hath since, by the stairs of his own deserts, climbed up to be a general, and now we come to character him.

He is pious in the ordering of his own life. Some falsely conceive that religion spoileth the spirit of a general, as bad as a rainy day doth his plume of feathers, making it droop and hang down; whereas, indeed, piety only begets true prowess.

He acknowledgeth God the Generalissimo of all armies, who in all battles, though the number be never so unequal, reserves the casting voice for himself. Yet can I scarce believe what one tells us, how Walter Pletemberg, master of the Teutonic Order, with a small number slew in a battle an hundred thousand Muscovite enemies, with the loss of but one man on his side.

He hath gained skill in his place by long experience; not beginning to lead others, before himself ever knew to follow, having never before (except in cock-matches) beheld any battles. Surely they leap best in their providence forward who fetch their rise farthest backward in their experience.

He either is, or is presumed valiant. Indeed, courage in him is necessary, though some think that a general is above valor who may command others to be so. As if it were all one whether courage were his naturally, or by adoption, who can make the valiant deeds of others seem his own; and his reputation for personal manhood, once raised, will bear itself up; like a round body, some force is required to set it, but a touch will keep it, agoing. Indeed, it is extreme indiscretion (except in extremities) for him to be prodigal of his person.

He is cheerful and willing in undergoing of labor. Admirable are the miracles of an industrious army: witness the mighty ditch in Cambridgeshire, made by the East-Angles, commonly called Devil's Ditch, as if the pioneers thereof came from hell. Thus the effeminateness of our age, defaming what it should imitate, falsely traduces the monuments of their ancestors' endeavors.

He loves, and is beloved of his soldiers; whose good will he attaineth,

1. By giving them good words in his speeches unto them. When wages have sometimes accidentally fallen short, soldiers have accepted the payment in the fair language and promises of their general.

2. By partaking with his soldiers in their painful employments. When the English, at the Spanish fleet's approach in eighty-eight, drew their ships out of Plymouth haven, the Lord Admiral Howard himself towed a cable, the least joint of whose exemplary hand drew more than twenty men besides.

3. By sharing with them in their wants. When victuals have grown scant, some generals have pinched themselves to the same fare with their soldiers, who could not complain that their mess was bad whilst their general was fellow-commoner with them.

4. By taking notice, and rewarding of their deserts; never disinheriting a worthy soldier of his birthright, of the next office due unto him. For a worthy man is wounded more deeply by his own general's neglect than by his enemy's sword; the latter may kill him, but

the former deads his courage, or, which is worse, mads it into discontent; who had rather others should make a ladder of his dead corpse to scale a city by it, than a bridge of him whilst alive for his punies to give him the go-by, and pass over him to preferment. For this reason chiefly (besides some others), a great and valiant English general in the days of Queen Elizabeth was hated of his soldiers, because he disposed offices by his own absolute will, without respect of orderly advancing such as deserved it, which made a great man once salute him with this letter: "Sir, if you will be pleased to bestow a captain's place on the bearer hereof, being a worthy gentleman, he shall do that for you which never as yet any soldier did, namely, pray to God for your health and happiness."

He is fortunate in what he undertakes. Such a one was Julius Cæsar, who, in Britain, a country undiscovered, peopled with a valiant nation, began a war in autumn, without apparent advantage, not having any intelligence there, being to pass over the sea into a colder climate, (an enterprise, saith one, well worthy the invincible courage of Cæsar, but not of his accustomed prudence,) and yet returned victorious. Indeed, God is the sole disposer of success; other gifts he also scattereth amongst men, yet so that they themselves scramble to gather them up; whereas success God gives immediately into their hands on whom he pleaseth to bestow it.

He trieth the forces of a new enemy before he encounters him. Samson is half conquered when it is known where his strength lies; and skirmishes are scouts for the discovery of the strength of an army before battle be given.

He makes his flying enemy a bridge of gold, and disarms them of their best weapon, which is, necessity to fight whether they will or no. Men forced to a battle against their intention often conquer beyond their expectation. Stop a flying coward, and he will turn his legs into arms, and lay about him manfully; whereas, open him a passage to escape, and he will quickly shut up his courage.

But I dare dwell no longer on this subject. When the Pope earnestly wrote to King Richard the First not to detain in prison his dear son, the martial bishop of Beauvais, the king sent the Pope back the armor wherein the bishop was taken with the words of Jacob's sons to their father, "See whether or no this be the coat of thy son." Surely, a corselet is no canonical coat for me, nor suits it with my clergy-profession to proceed any further in this warlike description.

THE GOOD SEA-CAPTAIN.

HIS military part is concurrent with that of the soldier already described: he differs only in some sea properties, which we will now set down. Conceive him now in a man-of-war, with his letters of mart, well armed, victualled, and appointed, and see how he acquits himself.

The more power he hath, the more careful he is not to abuse it. Indeed, a sea-captain is a king in the island of a ship, supreme judge, above appeal, in causes civil and criminal, and is seldom brought to an account in courts of justice on land for injuries done to his own men at sea.

He is careful in observing of the Lord's day. He hath a watch in his heart, though no bells in a steeple to proclaim that day by ringing to prayers. Sir Francis Drake, in three years' sailing about the world, lost one whole day, which was scarce considerable in so long time. 'T is to be feared some captains at sea lose a day every week, one in seven, neglecting the Sabbath.

He is as pious and thankful when a tempest is past, as devout when 't is present; not clamorous to receive mercies, and tongue-tied to return thanks. Many mariners are calm in a storm, and storm in a calm, blustering with oaths. In a tempest it comes to their turn to be religious, whose piety 's but a fit of the wind, and when that is allayed, their devotion is ended.

Escaping many dangers makes him not presumptuous to run into them. Not like those seamen who (as if their hearts were made of those rocks they have often sailed by) are so always in death they never think of it. These in their navigations observe that it is far hotter under the tropics in the coming to the line than under the line itself; and in like manner they conceive that the fear and fancy in preparing for death is more terrible than death itself, which makes them by degrees desperately to contemn it.

In taking a prize he most prizeth the men's lives whom he takes, though some of them may chance to be negroes or savages. It is the custom of some to cast them overboard, and there 's an end of them; for the dumb fishes will tell no tales. But the murder is not so soon drowned as the men. What! is a brother by half-blood no kin? A savage hath God to his father by creation, though not the Church to his mother, and God will revenge his innocent blood. But our captain counts the image of God nevertheless his image, cut in ebony as if done in ivory, and in the blackest Moors he sees the representation of the King of Heaven.

In dividing the gains, he wrongs none who took pains to get them; not shifting off his poor mariners with nothing, or giving them only the garbage of the prize, and keeping all the flesh to himself. In time of peace, he quietly returns home, and turns not to the trade of pirates, who are the worst sea-vermin, and the devil's water-rats.

His voyages are not only for profit, but some for honor and knowledge; to make discoveries of new countries, imitating the worthy Peter Columbus. Before his time the world was cut off at the middle, Hercules' Pillars (which indeed are the navel) being made the feet and utmost bounds of the continent, till his successful industry enlarged it.

"Primus ab infusis quod terra emerserat undis
Nuncius adveniens ipsa columba fuit.
Occiduis primus qui terram invenit in undis
Nuncius adveniens ipse Columbus erat."

Our sea-captain is likewise ambitious to perfect what the other began. He counts it a disgrace, seeing all mankind is one family, sundry countries but several rooms, that we who dwell in the parlor (so he counts Europe) should not know the outlodgings of the same house, and the world be scarce acquainted with itself before it be dissolved from itself at the day of judgment.

He daily sees and duly considers God's wonders in the deep. Tell me, ye naturalists, Who sounded the first march and retreat to the tide, "hither shalt thou come, and no further"? Why doth not the water recover his right over the earth, being higher in nature? Whence came the salt, and who first boiled it, which made so much brine? When the winds are not only wild in a storm, but even stark mad in a hurricane, who is it that restores them again to their wits, and brings them asleep in a calm? Who made the mighty whales, who swim in a sea of water, and have a sea of oil swimming in them? Who first taught the waters to imitate the creatures on land? so that the sea is the stable of horse-fishes, the stall of kine-fishes, the sty of hog-fishes, the kennel of dog-fishes, and in all things the sea the ape of the land. Whence grows the ambergris in the sea? which is not so hard to find where it is as to know what it is. Was not God the first shipwright? and all vessels on the water descended from the loins (or ribs rather) of Noah's ark? Or else who durst be so bold, with a few crooked boards nailed together, a stick standing upright, and a rag tied to it, to adventure into the ocean? What loadstone first touched the loadstone? or how first fell it in love with the north, rather affecting that cold climate than the pleasant east, or fruitful south, or west? How comes that stone to know more than men, and find the way to the land in a mist? In most of these, men take sanctuary at *occulta qualitas*, and complain that the room is dark, when their eyes are blind. Indeed, they are God's wonders; and that seaman the greatest wonder of all for his blockishness, who, seeing them daily, neither takes notice of them, admires at them, nor is thankful for them.

THE TRUE GENTLEMAN.

WE will consider him in his birth, breeding, and behavior.

He is extracted from ancient and worshipful parentage. When a pippin is planted on a pippin-stock, the fruit growing thence is called a renate, a most delicious apple, as both by sire and dam well descended. Thus his blood must needs be well purified who is gentilely born on both sides.

If his birth be not, at least his qualities are generous. What if he cannot with the Heveninghams of Suffolk count five-and-twenty knights of his family, or tell sixteen knights successively with the Tilneys of Norfolk, or with the Nauntons show where their ancestors had seven hundred pounds a year before or at the Conquest; yet he hath endeavored, by his own deserts, to ennoble himself. Thus valor makes him son to Cæsar, learning entitles him kinsman to Tully, and piety reports him nephew to godly Constantine. It graceth a gentleman of low descent and high desert, when he will own the meanness of his parentage. How ridiculous is it when many men brag that their families are more ancient than the moon, which all know are later than the star which some seventy years since shined in Cassiopea. But if he be generously born, see how his parents breed him.

He is not in his youth possessed with the great hopes of his possession. No flatterer reads constantly in his ears a survey of the lands he is to inherit. This hath made many boys' thoughts swell so great they could never be kept in compass afterwards. Only his parents acquaint him that he is the next undoubted heir to correction, if misbehaving himself; and he finds no more favor from his schoolmaster than his schoolmaster finds diligence in him, whose rod respects persons no more than bullets are partial in a battle.

At the university he is so studious as if he intended learning for his profession. He knows well that cunning is no burden to carry, as paying neither portage by land nor poundage by sea. Yea, though to have land be a good first, yet to have learning is the surest second, which may stand to it when the other may chance to be taken away.

At the inns of court he applies himself to learn the laws of the kingdom. Object not, "Why should a gentleman learn law, who, if he needeth it, may have it for his money, and if he hath never so much of his own, he must but give it away?" For what a shame is it for a man of quality to be ignorant of Solon in our Athens, of Lycurgus in our Sparta? Besides, law will help him to keep his own, and bestead his neighbors. Say not that there be enough which make this their set practice: for so there are also many masters of defence by their profession; and shall private men therefore learn no skill at their weapons?

As for the hospitality, the apparel, the travelling, the company, the recreations, the marriage of gentlemen, they are described in several chapters in the following book. A word or two of his behavior in the country.

He is courteous and affable to his neighbors. As the sword of the best tempered metal is most flexible, so the truly generous are most pliant and courteous in their behavior to their inferiors.

He delights to see himself and his servants well mounted: therefore he loveth good horsemanship. Let never any foreign Rabshakeh send that brave to our Jerusalem, offering to lend her two thousand horses, if she be able for her part to set riders upon them. We know how Darius got the Persian empire from the rest of his fellow-peers by the first neighing of his generous steed. It were no harm if, in some needless suits of intricate precedency betwixt equal gentlemen, the priority were adjudged to him who keeps a stable of most serviceable horses.

He furnisheth and prepareth himself in peace against time of war, lest it be too late to learn when his skill is to be used. He approves himself courageous when brought to the trial, as well remembering the custom which is used at the creation of Knights of the Bath, wherein the king's master-cook cometh forth, and presenteth his great knife to the new-made knights, admonishing them to be faithful and valiant, otherwise he threatens them that that very knife is prepared to cut off their spurs.

If the commission of the peace finds him out, he faithfully discharges it. I say, finds him out; for a public office is a guest which receives the best usage from them who never invited it. And though he declined the place, the country knew to prize his worth, who would be ignorant of his own. He compounds many petty differences betwixt his neighbors, which are easier ended in his own porch than in Westminster Hall: for many people think, if once they have fetched a warrant from a justice, they have given earnest to follow the suit, though otherwise the matter be so mean that the next night's sleep would have bound both parties to the peace, and made them as good friends as ever before. Yet

He connives not at the smothering of punishable faults. He hates that practice, as common as dangerous amongst country people, who, having received again the goods which were stolen from them, partly out of foolish pity, and partly out of covetousness to save charges in prosecuting the law, let the thief escape unpunished. Thus, whilst private losses are repaired, the wounds to the commonwealth (in the breach of the laws) are left uncured; and thus petty larceners are encouraged into felons, and afterwards are hanged for pounds, because never whipped for pence, who, if they had felt the cord, had never been brought to the halter.

If chosen a member of Parliament, he is willing to do his country service. If he be no rhetorician to raise affections, (yea, Mercury was a greater speaker than Jupiter himself,) he counts it great wisdom to be the good manager of yea and nay. The slow pace of his judgment is recompensed by the swift following of his affections, when his judgment is once soundly informed. And here we leave him in consultation, wishing him, with the rest of his honorable society, all happy success.

THE VIRTUOUS LADY.

TO describe a holy state without a virtuous lady therein, were to paint out a year without a spring: we come therefore to her character.

She sets not her face so often by her glass as she composeth her soul by God's word,—which hath all the excellent qualities of a glass indeed.

1. It is clear; in all points necessary to salvation, except to such whose eyes are blinded.

2. It is true; not like those false glasses some ladies dress themselves by. And how common is flattery, when even glasses have learnt to be parasites!

3. It is large; presenting all spots *cap-a-pie* behind and before, within and without.

4. It is durable; though in one sense it is broken too often (when God's laws are neglected), yet it will last to break them that break it, and one tittle thereof shall not fall to the ground.

5. This glass hath power to smooth the

wrinkles, cleanse the spots, and mend the faults it discovers.

She walks humbly before God in all religious duties. Humbly; for she well knows that the strongest Christian is like the city of Rome, which was never besieged but it was taken; and the best saint without God's assistance would be as often foiled as tempted. She is most constant and diligent at her hours of private prayer. Queen Catharine Dowager never kneeled on a cushion when she was at her devotions: this matters not at all; our lady is more careful of her heart than of her knees, that her soul be settled aright.

She is careful and most tender of her credit and reputation. There is a tree in Mexicana which is so exceedingly tender that a man cannot touch any of his branches but it withers presently. A lady's credit is of equal niceness: a small touch may wound and kill it; which makes her very cautious what company she keeps. The Latin tongue seems somewhat injurious to the feminine sex; for whereas therein *amicus* is a friend, *amica* always signifies a sweetheart; as if their sex in reference to men were not capable of any other kind of familiar friendship but in way to marriage: which makes our lady avoid all privacy with suspicious company.

Yet is she not more careful of her own

credit than of God's glory; and stands up valiantly in the defence thereof. She hath read how, at the coronation of King Richard the Second, Dame Margaret Dimock, wife to Sir John Dimock, came into the court and claimed the place to be the king's champion by the virtue of the tenure of her manor of Scrinelby in Lincolnshire, to challenge and defy all such as opposed the king's right to the crown. But if our lady hears any speaking disgracefully of God or religion, she counts herself bound by her tenure (whereby she holds possession of grace here, and reversion of glory hereafter) to assert and vindicate the honor of the King of Heaven, whose champion she professeth to be. One may be a lamb in private wrongs, but in hearing general affronts to goodness, they are asses which are not lions.

She is pitiful and bountiful to people in distress. We read how a daughter of the Duke of Exeter invented a brake or cruel rack to torment people withal, to which purpose it was long reserved, and often used in the Tower of London, and commonly called (was it not fit so pretty a babe should bear her mother's name?) the Duke of Exeter's Daughter. Methinks the finding out of a salve to ease poor people in pain had borne better proportion to her ladyship than to have been the inventor of instruments of cruelty.

She is a good scholar, and well learned in useful authors. Indeed, as in purchases a house is valued at nothing, because it returneth no profit and requires great charges to maintain it, so, for the same reasons, learning in a woman is but little to be prized. But as for great ladies, who ought to be a confluence of all rarities and perfections, some learning in them is not only useful, but necessary.

In discourse, her words are rather fit than fine, very choice and yet not chosen. Though her language be not gaudy, yet the plainness thereof pleaseth, — it is so proper, and handsomely put on. Some, having a set of fine phrases, will hazard an impertinency to use them all, as thinking they give full satisfaction, for dragging in the matter by head and shoulders, if they dress it in quaint expressions. Others often repeat the same things, the Platonic year of their discourses being not above three days long, in which term all the same matter returns over again, threadbare talk, ill suiting with the variety of their clothes.

She affects not the vanity of foolish fashions; but is decently apparelled according to her state and condition. He that should have guessed the bigness of Alexander's soldiers by their shields left in India would much over-proportion their true greatness. But what a vast overgrown creature would some guess a woman to be, taking his aim by the multitude and variety of clothes and ornaments which some of them use: insomuch as the ancient Latins called a woman's wardrobe *mundus*, a world; wherein notwithstanding was much *terra incognita*, then undiscovered, but since found out by the curiosity of modern fashion-mongers. We find a map of this world drawn by God's spirit, *Isaiah* iii. 18, wherein one-and-twenty women's ornaments (all superfluous) are reckoned up, which at this day are much increased. The moons, there mentioned, which they wore on their heads, may seem since grown to the full in the luxury of after-ages.

She is contented with that beauty which God hath given her. If very handsome, no whit the more proud, but far the more thankful: if unhandsome, she labors to better it in the virtues of her mind; that what is but plain cloth without may be rich plush within. Indeed such natural defects as hinder her comfortable serving of God in her calling may be amended by art; and any member of the body being defective, may thereby be lawfully supplied. Thus glass eyes may be used, though not for seeing, for sightliness. But our lady detesteth all adulterate complexions, finding no precedent thereof in the Bible save one, and her so bad that ladies would blush through their paint to make her the pattern of their imitation. Yet are there many that think the grossest fault in painting is to paint grossly, (making their faces with thick daubing not only new pictures, but new statues,) and that the greatest sin therein is to be discovered.

In her marriage she principally respects virtue and religion, and next that, other accommodations, as we have formerly discoursed of. And she is careful in match, not to bestow herself unworthily beneath her own degree to an ignoble person, except in case of necessity. Thus the gentlewomen in Champagne in France, some three hundred years since, were enforced to marry yeomen and farmers, because all the nobility in that country were slain in the wars, in the two voyages of King Louis to Palestine; and thereupon ever since, by custom and privilege, the gentlewomen of Champagne and Brie ennoble their husbands, and give them honor in marrying them, how mean soever before.

Though pleasantly affected, she is not transported with court-delights; as in their stately masques and pageants. By degrees she is brought from delighting in such masques, only to be contented to see them, and at last, perchance, could desire to be excused from that also.

Yet in her reduced thoughts she makes all the sport she hath seen earnest to herself: it must be a dry flower indeed out of which this bee sucks no honey: they are the best Origens who do allegorize all earthly vanities into heavenly truths. When she remembereth how suddenly the scene in the masque was altered (almost before moment itself could take notice of it), she considereth how quickly mutable all things are in this world, God ringing the changes on all accidents, and making them tunable to his glory: the lively representing of things so curiously that nature herself might grow jealous of art in outdoing her, minds our lady to make sure work with her own soul, seeing hypocrisy may be so like to sincerity. But oh, what a wealthy exchequer of beauties did she there behold, several faces most different, most excellent, (so great is the variety even in bests,) what a rich mine of jewels above-ground, all so brave, so costly! To give court-masques their due, of all the bubbles in this world they have the greatest variety of fine colors. But all is quickly ended: this is the spite of the world, — if ever she affordeth fine ware, she always pincheth it in the measure, and it lasts not long. But oh, thinks our lady, how glorious a place is heaven, where there are joys for evermore. If a herd of kine should meet together to fancy and define happiness, they would place it to consist in fine pastures, sweet grass, clear water, shadowy groves, constant summer; but if any winter, then warm shelter and dainty hay, with company after their kind, counting these low things the highest happiness because their conceit can reach no higher. Little better do the heathen poets describe heaven, paving it with pearl, and roofing it with stars, filling it with gods and goddesses, and allowing them to drink (as if without it no poet's paradise) nectar and ambrosia; heaven indeed being *poetarum dedecus*, the shame of poets, and the disgrace of all their hyperboles falling as far short of truth herein as they go beyond it in other fables. However, the sight of such glorious earthly spectacles advantageth our lady's conceit by infinite multiplication thereof to consider of heaven.

She reads constant lectures to herself of her own mortality. To smell to a turf of fresh earth is wholesome for the body; no less are thoughts of mortality cordial to the soul. "Earth thou art, to earth thou shalt return." The sight of death when it cometh will neither be so terrible to her, nor so strange, who hath formerly often beheld it in her serious meditations. With Job she saith to the worm, "Thou art my sister." If fair ladies scorn to own the worms their kindred in this life, their kindred will be bold to challenge them when dead in their graves; for when the soul (the best perfume of the body) is departed from it, it becomes so noisome a carcass, that, should I make a description of the loathsomeness thereof, some dainty dames would hold their noses in reading it.

To conclude: we read how Henry, a German prince, was admonished by revelation to search for a writing in an old wall, which should nearly concern him, wherein he found only these two words written, POST SEX, *after six.* Whereupon Henry conceived that his death was foretold, which after six days should ensue; which made him pass those days in constant preparation for the same. But finding the six days past without the effect he expected, he successively persevered in his godly resolutions six weeks, six months, six years, and on the first day of the seventh year the prophecy was fulfilled, though otherwise than he interpreted it; for thereupon he was chosen Emperor of Germany, having before gotten such a habit of piety that he persisted in his religious course forever after. Thus our lady hath so inured herself "all the days of her appointed time to wait till her change cometh," that, expecting it every hour, she is always provided for that than which nothing is more certain or uncertain.

THE WISE STATESMAN.

TO describe the statesman at large is the subject rather of a volume than a chapter, and is as far beyond my power as wide of my profession. We will not launch into the deep, but satisfy ourselves to sail by the shore, and briefly observe his carriage towards God, his king, himself, home-persons, and foreign princes.

He counts the fear of God the beginning of wisdom; and therefore esteemeth no project profitable which is not lawful; nothing politic which crosseth piety. Let not any plead for the contrary, Hushai's dealing with Absalom, which strongly savored of double-dealing; for what is a question cannot be an argument, seeing the lawfulness of his deed therein was never decided; and he is unwise that will venture the state of his soul on the litigious title of such an example. Besides, we must live by God's precepts, not by the godly's practice. And though God causeth sometimes the sun of success to shine as well on bad as good projects, yet commonly wicked actions end in shame at the last.

In giving counsel to his prince, he had rather displease than hurt him. Plain dealing is one of the daintiest rarities can be presented to some princes, as being novelty to them all times of the year. The philosopher could say, *Quid omnia possidentibus deest? Ille qui verum dicat.* Wherefore our statesman seeks to undeceive his prince from the fallacies of flatterers, who by their plausible persuasions have bolstered up their crooked counsels, to make them seem straight in the king's eyes.

He is constant, but not obstinate in the advice he gives. Some think it beneath a wise man to alter their opinion: a maxim both false and dangerous. We know what worthy father wrote his own retractation; and it matters not though we go back from our word, so we go forward in the truth and a sound judgment. Such a one changeth not his main opinion; which ever was this, to embrace that course which, upon mature deliberation, shall appear unto him the most advised. As for his carriage towards himself,

He taketh an exact survey of his own defects and perfections. As for the former, his weaknesses and infirmities he doth carefully and wisely conceal: sometimes he covers them over with a cautious confidence, and presents a fair hilt, but keeps the sword in the sheath, which wanteth an edge. But this he manageth with much art; otherwise, being betrayed, it would prove most ridiculous, and it would make brave music to his enemies to hear the hissing of an empty bladder when it is pricked.

His known perfections he seeks modestly to cloud and obscure. It is needless to show the sun shining, which will break out of itself. Not like our fantastics, who, having a fine watch, draw all occasions to draw it out to be seen. Yea, because sometimes he concealeth his sufficiency in such things wherein others know he hath ability, he shall therefore be thought at other times to have ability in those matters wherein indeed he wants it, men interpreting him therein rather modestly to dissemble than to be defective. Yet, when just occasion is offered, he shows his perfections soundly, though seldom, and then graceth them out to the best advantage.

In discourse, he is neither too free nor over-reserved, but observes a mediocrity. His hall is common to all comers, but his closet is locked. General matters he is as liberal to impart as careful to conceal importancies. Moderate liberty in speech inviteth and provoketh liberty to be used again, where a constant closeness makes all suspect him; and his company is burdensome that liveth altogether on the expenses of others, and will lay out nothing himself. Yea, who will barter intelligence with him that returns no considerable ware in exchange?

He trusteth not any with a secret which may endanger his estate. For if he tells it to his servant, he makes him his master; if to his friend, he enables him to be a foe, and to undo him at pleasure, whose secrecy he must buy at the party's own price; and if ever he shuts his purse, the other opens his mouth. Matters of inferior consequence he will communicate to a fast friend, and crave his advice; for two eyes see more than one, though it be never so big, and set (as in Polyphemus) in the midst of the forehead.

He is careful and provident in the managing of his private estate. Excellently Ambrose, *An idoneum putabo qui mihi det consilium, qui non dat sibi?* Well may princes suspect those statesmen not to be wise in the business of the commonwealth who are fools in ordering their own affairs. Our politician, if he enlargeth not his own estate, at least keeps it in good repair. As for avaricious courses, he disdaineth them. Sir Thomas More, though some years Lord Chancellor of England, scarce left his son five-and-twenty pounds a year more than his father left him. And Sir Henry Sidney (father to Sir Philip), being Lord President of Wales and Ireland, got not one foot of land in either country, rather seeking after the common good than his private profit. I must confess the last age produced an English statesman, who was the pick-lock of the cabinets of foreign princes, who, though the wisest in his time and way, died poor and indebted to private men, though not so much as the whole kingdom was indebted to him. But such an accident is rare; and a small hospital will hold those statesmen who have impaired their means, not by their private carelessness, but carefulness for the public. As for his carriage towards home-persons,

He studieth men's natures, first reading the title-pages of them by the report of fame, but credits not fame's relations to the full. Otherwise, as in London Exchange one shall over-buy wares who gives half the price at first demanded, so he that believeth the moiety of fame may believe too much. Wherefore, to be more accurate,

He reads the chapters of men's natures (chiefly his concurrents and competitors) by the reports of their friends and foes, making allowance for their engagements, not believing all in the mass, but only what he judiciously extracteth. Yet virtues confessed by their foes, and vices acknowledged by their friends, are commonly true. The best intelligence, if it can be obtained, is from a fugitive privado.

But the most legible character and truest edition wherein he reads a man, is in his own occasional openings; and that in these three cases: —

1. When the party discloses himself in his wine; for though it be unlawful to practise on any to make them drunk, yet no doubt one

may make a good use of another man's abusing himself. What they say of the herb *lunaria*, ceremoniously gathered at some set times, that, laid upon any lock, it makes it fly open, is most true of drunkenness, unbolting the most important secrets.

2. When he discovereth himself in his passions. Physicians, to make some small veins in their patients' arms plump and full, that they may see them the better to let them blood, use to put them into hot water: so the heat of passion presenteth many invisible veins in men's hearts to the eye of the beholder; yea, the sweat of anger washeth off their paint, and makes them appear in their true colors.

3. When accidentally they bolt out speeches unawares to themselves. More hold is then to be taken of a few words casually uttered, than of set, solemn speeches, which rather show men's arts than their natures, as indited rather from their brains than hearts. The drop of one word may show more than the stream of a whole oration; and our statesman, by examining such fugitive passages (which have stolen on a sudden out of the party's mouth), arrives at his best intelligence.

In court-factions he keeps himself in a free neutrality. Otherwise to engage himself needlessly were both folly and danger. When Francis the First, King of France, was consulting with his captains how to lead his army over the Alps into Italy, whether this way or that way, Amarill, his fool, sprang out of a corner, where he sat unseen, and bade them rather take care which way they should bring their army out of Italy back again. Thus is it easy for one to interest and embark himself in others' quarrels, but much difficulty it is to be disengaged from them afterwards. Nor will our statesman entitle himself a party in any feminine discords, knowing that women's jars breed men's wars.

Yet he counts neutrality profaneness in such matters wherein God, his prince, the Church, or State are concerned. Indeed, "he that meddleth with strife not belonging unto him is like one that taketh a dog by the ears." Yet, if the dog worrieth a sheep, we may, yea, ought to rescue it from his teeth, and must be champions for innocence when it is overborne with might. He that will stand neuter in such matters of moment, wherein his calling commands him to be a party, with Servilius in Rome, will please neither side; of whom the historian says, *P. Servilius medium se gerendo, nec plebis vitavit odium, nec apud patres gratiam inivit.* And just it is with God, that they should be strained in the twist who stride so wide as to set their legs in two opposite sides. Indeed, an upright shoe may fit both feet, but I never saw a glove that would serve both hands. Neutrality in matters of an indifferent nature may fit well, but never suit well in important matters, of far different conditions.

He is the centre wherein lines of intelligence meet from all foreign countries. He is careful that his outlandish instructions be full, true, and speedy; not with the sluggard telling for news at noon that the sun is risen. But more largely hereof in the Ambassador, hereafter.

He refuseth all underhand pensions from foreign princes. Indeed, honorary rewards received with the approbation of his sovereign, may be lawful, and less dangerous. For, although even such gifts tacitly oblige him by way of gratitude to do all good offices to that foreign prince whose pensioner he is, yet his counsels pass not but with an open abatement in regard of his known engagements; and so the State is armed against the advice of such who are well known to lean to one side. But secret pensions, which flow from foreign princes, like the River Anas in Spain, underground, not known or discerned, are most mischievous. The receivers of such will play under-board at the council-table; and the eating and digesting of such outlandish food will by degrees fill their veins with outlandish blood, even in their very hearts.

His masterpiece is in negotiating for his own

master with foreign princes. At Rhodes there was a contention betwixt Apelles and Protogenes, corrivals in the mystery of limning. Apelles, with his pencil, drew a very slender even line; Protogenes drew another, more small and slender, in the midst thereof with another color; Apelles again, with a third line of a different color, drew through the midst of that Protogenes had made, *nullum relinquens amplius subtilitati locum.* Thus our statesman traverseth matters, doubling and redoubling in his foreign negotiations with the politicians of other princes, winding and intrenching themselves mutually within the thoughts each of other, till at last our statesman leaves no degrees of subtilty to go beyond him.

To conclude, some plead that dissembling is lawful in state-craft, upon the presupposition that men must meet with others which dissemble. Yea, they hold, that thus to counterfeit, *se defendendo*, against a crafty corrival, is no sin, but a just punishment on our adversary, who first began it. And therefore statesmen sometimes must use crooked shoes to fit hurled feet. Besides, the honest politician would quickly be beggared, if, receiving black money from cheaters, he pays them in good silver, and not in their own coin back again. For my part, I confess that herein I rather see what than whither to fly; neither able to answer their arguments, nor willing to allow their practice. But what shall I say? They need to have steady heads who can dive into these gulfs of policy, and come out with a safe conscience. I will look no longer on these whirlpools of state, lest my pen turn giddy.

THE AMBASSADOR.

HE is one that represents his king in a foreign country (as a deputy doth in his own dominions) under the assurance of the public faith, authorized by the law of nations. He is either extraordinary, for some one affair, with time limited; or, ordinary, for general matters, during his prince's pleasure, commonly called a legier.

He is born, made, or at leastwise qualified honorably, both for the honor of the sender and him to whom he is sent; especially if the solemnity of the action wherein he is employed consisteth in ceremony and magnificence. Louis the Eleventh, King of France, is sufficiently condemned by posterity for sending Oliver, his barber, in an embassage to a princess, who so trimly despatched his business that he left it in the suds, and had been well washed in the river at Ghent for his pains, if his feet had not been the more nimble.

He is of a proper, at least passable, person. Otherwise, if he be of a contemptible presence, he is absent whilst he is present; especially if employed in love-businesses to advance a marriage. Ladies will dislike the body for a deformed shadow. The jest is well known: when the State of Rome sent two ambassadors, the one having scars on his head, the other lame in his feet, *mittit populus Romanus legationem quæ nec caput habet, nec pedes*, the people of Rome send an embassy without head or feet.

He hath a competent estate whereby to maintain his port: for a great poverty is ever suspected; and he that hath a breach in his estate, lies open to be assaulted with bribes. Wherefore his means ought at least to be sufficient, both to defray set and constant charges, as also to make sallies and excursions of expenses on extraordinary occasions, which we may call supererogations of state. Otherwise, if he be indigent and succeed a bountiful predecessor, he will seem a fallow field after a plentiful crop.

He is a passable scholar, well travelled in countries and histories; well studied in the pleas of the crown, I mean not such as are at home, betwixt his sovereign and his subjects, but abroad betwixt his and foreign princes; to this end he is well skilled in the imperial laws. Common law itself is outlawed beyond the seas; which though a most true, is too short a measure of right, and reacheth not foreign kingdoms.

He well understandeth the language of that country to which he is sent; and yet he desires rather to seem ignorant of it, (if such a simulation, which stands neuter betwixt a truth and a lie, be lawful,) and that for these reasons: first, because though he can speak it never so exactly, his eloquence therein will be but stammering, compared to the ordinary talk of the natives: secondly, hereby he shall in a manner stand invisible, and view others; and as Joseph's deafness heard all the dialogues betwixt his brethren, so his not owning to understand the language shall expose their talk the more open unto him: thirdly, he shall have the more advantage to speak and negotiate in his own language; at the leastwise, if he cannot make them come over to him, he may meet them in the midway, in the Latin, a speech common to all learned nations.

He gets his commission and instructions well ratified and confirmed before he sets forth. Otherwise it is the worst prison to be commission-bound. And seeing he must not jet out the least penthouse beyond his foundation, he had best well survey the extent of his authority.

He furnisheth himself with fit officers in his family. Especially he is careful in choosing

1. A secretary, honest and able, careful to conceal counsels, and not such a one as will let drop out of his mouth whatsoever is poured in at his ear: yea, the head of every ambassador sleeps on the breast of his secretary.

2. A steward, wise and provident, such as can temper magnificence with moderation, judiciously fashioning his ordinary expenses with his master's estate, reserving a spare for all events and accidental occasions, and making all things to pass with decency, without any rudeness, noise, or disorder.

He seasonably presents his embassage, and demands audience. Such is the fresh nature of some embassages, if not spent presently, they scent ill. Thus it is ridiculous to condole griefs almost forgotten; for (besides that with a cruel courtesy it makes their sorrows bleed afresh) it foolishly seems to teach one to take that which he hath formerly digested. When some Trojan ambassadors came to comfort Tiberius Cæsar for the loss of his son, dead wellnigh a twelvemonth before; "And I," said the emperor, "am very sorry for your grief for the death of your Hector, slain by Achilles a thousand years since."

Coming to have audience, he applieth himself only to the prince to whom he is sent. When Chancellor Morville, ambassador from the French king, delivering his message to Philip, Duke of Burgundy, was interrupted by Charles, the Duke's son, "I am sent," said he, "not to treat with you, but with your father." And our Mr. Wade is highly commended, that, being sent by Queen Elizabeth to Philip, King of Spain, he would not be turned over to the Spanish Privy Council, (whose greatest grandees were dwarfs in honor to his queen,) but would either have audience from the king himself, or would return without it. And yet afterwards our ambassador knows (if desirous that his business should take effect) how and when to make his secret and underhand addresses to such potent favorites as strike the stroke in the State; it often happening in commonwealths that the master's mate steers the ship thereof more than the master himself.

In delivering his message, he complies with the garb and guise of the country; either longer, briefer, more plain, or more flourishing, as it is most acceptable to such to whom he directs his speech. The Italians (whose country is called "the country of good words") love the circuits of courtesy, that an ambassador should not, as a sparrow-hawk, fly outright to his prey, and meddle presently with the matter in hand; but with the noble falcon, mount in language, soar high, fetch compasses of compliment, and then in due time stoop to game and seize on the business propounded. Clean contrary the Switzers (who sent word to the King of France, not to send them an ambassador with store of words, but a treasurer with plenty of money) count all words quite out which are not straight on, have an antipathy against eloquent language; the flowers of rhetoric being as offensive to them as sweet perfumes to such as are troubled with the mother. Yea, generally, great soldiers have their stomachs sharp set to feed on the matter, loathing long speeches, as wherein they conceive themselves to lose time in which they could conquer half a country, and, counting bluntness their best eloquence, love to be accosted in their own kind.

He commands himself not to admire anything presented unto him. He looks, but not gazeth on foreign magnificence, (as country clowns on a city,) beholding them with a familiar eye, as challenging old acquaintance, having known them long before. If he be surprised with a sudden wonder, he so orders it, that, though his soul within feels an admiration, none can perceive it without in his countenance. For,

1. It is inconsistent with the steadiness of his gravity to be startled with a wonder.

2. Admiration is the daughter of ignorance: whereas he ought to be so read in the world as to be posed with no rarity.

3. It is a tacit confession (if he wonders at state, strength, or wealth) that herein his own master's kingdom is far surpassed. And yet he will not slight and neglect such worthy sights as he beholds, which would savor too much of sullenness and self-addiction, things ill beseeming his noble spirit.

He is zealous of the least punctilios of his master's honor. Herein 't is most true, the law of honor *servanda in apicibus*: yea, a toy may be real, and a point may be essential to the sense of some sentences, and worse to be spared than some whole letter. Great kings wrestle together by the strength and nimbleness of their ambassadors; wherefore ambassadors are careful to afford no advantage to the adverse party; and mutually no more hold is given than what is gotten, lest the fault of the ambassador be drawn into precedent, to the prejudice of his master. He that abroad will lose an hair of his king's honor, deserves to lose his own head when he comes home.

He appears not violent in desiring anything he would effect; but with a seeming carelessness most carefully advanceth his master's business. If employed to conclude a peace, he represents his master as indifferent therein for his own part, but that desiring to spare Christian blood, preponderates him for peace, whose conscience, not purse or arms, are weary of the war: he entreats not, but treats for an accord, for their mutual good. But if the ambassador declareth himself zealous for it, perchance he may be forced to buy those conditions which otherwise would be given him.

He is constantly and certainly informed of all passages in his own country. What a shame is it for him to be a stranger to his native affairs! Besides, if gulls and rumors from his country be raised on purpose to amuse our ambassador, he rather smiles than starts at these false vizards, who, by private instructions from home, knows the true face of his country-estate. And lest his master's secretary should fail him herein, he counts it thrift to cast away some pounds yearly to some private friend in the court, to send him true information of all home-remarkables.

He carefully returns good intelligence to his master that employeth him.

1. Speedy; not being such a sluggard as to write for news at noon, that the sun is risen.

2. True; so far forth as may be; else he stamps it with a mark of uncertainty or suspicion.

3. Full; not filling the paper, but informing those to whom it is written.

4. Material; not grinding his advices too small, to frivolous particulars of love-toys, and private brawls, as one layeth it to the charge of Francis Guicciardine's History,—*Minutissima quæque narrat, parum ex lege aut dignitate historiæ.* And yet such particulars, which are too mean to be served up to the council-table, may make a feast for ladies, or other his friends; and therefore to such our ambassador relates them by his private letters.

5. Methodical; not running on all in a continued strain, but stopping at the stages of different businesses to breathe himself and the reader, and to take and begin a new sentence.

6. Well penned, clear and plain; not hunting after language, but teaching words their distance to wait on his matter, intermingling sententious speeches sparingly, lest seeming affected. And if constrained twice to write the same matter, still he varieth his words, lest he may seem to write like notaries, by precedents.

He will not have his house serve as a retreating-place for people suspected and odious in that State wherein he is employed. Much less shall his house be a sanctuary for offenders, seeing the very horns of God's altar did push away from them such notorious malefactors as did fly unto them for protection.

He is cautious not to practise any treacherous act against the prince under whom he lives; lest the shield of his embassy prove too small to defend him from the sword of justice, seeing that for such an offence an ambassador is resolved into a private man, and may worthily be punished, as in the cases of Bernardinus Mendoza and the Bishop of Ross. Yea, he will not so much as break forth publicly into any discourse, which he knows will be distasteful in that country wherein he is employed. Learned Bodin, who some seventy years since waited on Monsieur into England, was here, though highly admired for his learning, condemned much for his indiscretion, if his corrival's pen may be credited. For being feasted at an English lord's table, he fell into the odious discourse, that a princess, meaning Mary Queen of Scots, was, after Queen Elizabeth, the presumptive inheritrix of the English crown, notwithstanding an English law seemed to exclude those who are born out of the land; "And yet," said he, "I know not where this law is, for all the diligence that I have used to find it out." To whom it was suddenly replied by the lord that entertained him, "You shall find it written on the backside of your Salic law:" a judicious and biting rebound.

He is careful of suspicious complying with that prince to whom he is sent; as to receive from him any extraordinary gifts, much less pensions, which carry with them more than an appearance of evil. Sir Amias Paulet was so scrupulous herein, that, being ambassador in France in the days of Queen Elizabeth, he would not at his departure receive from the French king the chain of gold (which is given of course) till he was half a league out of the city of Paris.

If he hath any *libera mandata*, unlimited instructions, herein his discretion is most admirable.

But what go I about to do? Hereof enough already, if not too much; it better complying with my profession to practise St. Paul's precept to mine own parishioners, "Now then we are ambassadors for Christ, as though God did beseech you by us, we pray you, in Christ's stead, be reconciled to God."

THE HOLY STATE.

OF HOSPITALITY.

HOSPITALITY is threefold: for one's family; this is of necessity: for strangers; this is courtesy: for the poor; this is charity. Of the two latter.

To keep a disorderly house is the way to keep neither house nor lands. For whilst they keep the greatest roaring, their state steals away in the greatest silence. Yet, when many consume themselves with secret vices, then hospitality bears the blame: whereas, it is not the meat but the sauce, not the supper but the gaming after it, doth undo them.

Measure not thy entertainment of a guest by his estate, but thine own. Because he is a lord, forget not that thou art but a gentleman: otherwise, if with feasting him thou breakest thyself, he will not cure thy rupture, and (perchance) rather deride than pity thee.

When provision (as we say) groweth on the

same, it is miraculously multiplied. In Northamptonshire all the rivers of the county are bred in it, besides those (Ouse and Charwell) it lendeth and sendeth into other shires: so the good housekeeper hath a fountain of wheat in his field, mutton in his fold, &c., both to serve himself and supply others. The expense of a feast will but breathe him, which will tire another of the same estate who buys all by the penny.

Mean men's palates are best pleased with fare rather plentiful than various, solid than dainty. Dainties will cost more, and content less, to those that are not critical enough to distinguish them.

Occasional entertainment of men greater than thyself is better than solemn inviting them. Then short warning is thy large excuse: whereas, otherwise, if thou dost not overdo thy estate, thou shalt underdo his expectation; for thy feast will be but his ordinary fare. A king of France was often pleased in his hunting wilfully to lose himself, to find the house of a private park-keeper; where, going from the school of state-affairs, he was pleased to make a play-day to himself. He brought sauce (hunger) with him, which made coarse meat dainties to his palate. At last the park-keeper took heart, and solemnly invited the king to his house, who came with all his court, so that all the man's meat was not a morsel for them. "Well," said the park-keeper, "I will invite no more kings;" having learnt the difference between princes when they please to put on the vizard of privacy, and when they will appear like themselves, both in their person and attendants.

Those are ripe for charity which are withered by age or impotency, especially if maimed in following their calling; for such are industry's martyrs, at least her confessors. Add to these those that with diligence fight against poverty, though neither conquer till death make it a drawn battle. Expect not, but prevent their craving of thee; for God forbid the heavens should never rain till the earth first opens her mouth, seeing some grounds will sooner burn than chap.

The house of correction is the fittest hospital for those cripples whose legs are lame through their own laziness. Surely, King Edward the Sixth was as truly charitable in granting Bridewell for the punishment of sturdy rogues as in giving St. Thomas's Hospital for the relief of the poor. I have done with the subject; only I desire rich men to awaken hospitality, which one saith since the year 1572 hath in a manner been laid asleep in the grave of Edward, Earl of Derby.

OF JESTING.

HARMLESS mirth is the best cordial against the consumption of the spirits: wherefore jesting is not unlawful if it trespasseth not in quantity, quality, or season.

It is good to make a jest, but not to make a trade of jesting. The Earl of Leicester, knowing that Queen Elizabeth was much delighted to see a gentleman dance well, brought the master of a dancing-school to dance before her. "Pish," said the Queen, "it is his profession; I will not see him." She liked it not where it was a master-quality, but where it attended on other perfections. The same may we say of jesting.

Jest not with the two-edged sword of God's word. Will nothing please thee to wash thy hands in but the font? or to drink healths in but the church chalice? And know the whole art is learnt at the first admission, and profane jests will come without calling. If, in the troublesome days of King Edward the Fourth, a citizen in Cheapside was executed as a traitor for saying he would make his son heir to the crown, though he only meant his own house, having a crown for the sign; more dangerous it is to wit-wanton it with the majesty of God. Wherefore, if without thine intention, and against thy will, by chance-medley thou hittest Scripture in ordinary discourse, yet fly to the city of refuge, and pray to God to forgive thee.

Wanton jests make fools laugh, and wise men frown. Seeing we are civilized Englishmen, let us not be naked savages in our talk. Such rotten speeches are worst in withered age, when men run after that sin in their words which flieth from them in the deed.

Let not thy jests, like mummy, be made of dead men's flesh. Abuse not any that are departed; for to wrong their memories is to rob their ghosts of their winding-sheets.

Scoff not at the natural defects of any which are not in their power to amend. Oh, 't is cruelty to beat a cripple with his own crutches. Neither flout any for his profession, if honest, though poor and painful. Mock not a cobbler for his black thumbs.

He that relates another man's wicked jest with delight, adopts it to be his own. Purge them therefore from their poison. If the profaneness may be severed from the wit, it is like a lamprey; take out the string in the back, it may make good meat: but if the staple conceit consists in profaneness, then it is a viper, all poison, and meddle not with it.

He that will lose his friend for a jest, deserves to die a beggar by the bargain. Yet some think their conceits, like mustard, not good except they bite. We read that all those who were born in England the year after the beginning of the great mortality, 1349, wanted their four cheek-teeth. Such let thy jests be, that they may not grind the credit of thy friend, and make not jests so long till thou becomest one.

No time to break jests when the heart-strings are about to be broken. No more showing of wit when the head is to be cut off. Like that dying man, who, when the priest coming to him to give him extreme unction, asked of him where his feet were, answered, "At the end of my legs." But at such a time jests are an unmannerly *crepitus ingenii:* and let those take heed who end here with Democritus, that they begin not with Heraclitus hereafter.

OF SELF-PRAISING.

HE whose own worth doth speak, need not speak his own worth. Such boasting sounds proceed from emptiness of desert: whereas the conquerors in the Olympian games did not put on the laurels on their own heads, but waited till some other did it. Only anchorets that want company may crown themselves with their own commendations.

It showeth more wit but no less vanity to commend one's self not in a straight line but by reflection. Some sail to the port of their own praise by a side-wind; as when they dispraise themselves, stripping themselves naked of what is their due, that the modesty of the beholders may clothe them with it again; or when they flatter another to his face, tossing the ball to him that he may throw it back again to them; or when they commend that quality, wherein themselves excel, in another man (though absent) whom all know far their inferior in that faculty; or, lastly, (to omit other ambushes men set to surprise praise,) when they send the children of their own brain to be nursed by another man, and commend their own works in a third person, but if challenged by the company that they were authors of them themselves, with their tongues they faintly deny it, and with their faces strongly affirm it.

Self-praising comes most naturally from a man when it comes most violently from him in his own defence. For though modesty binds a man's tongue to the peace in this point, yet, being assaulted in his credit, he may stand upon his guard, and then he doth not so much praise as purge himself. One braved a gentleman to his face that in skill and valor he came far behind him. "'T is true," said the other, "for when I fought with you, you ran away before me." In such a case, it was well returned, and without any just aspersion of pride.

He that falls into sin is a man; that grieves at it, is a saint; that boasteth of it, is a devil. Yet some glory in their shame, counting the stains of sin the best complexion for their souls. These men make me believe it may be true what Mandeville writes of the Isle of Somabarre, in the East Indies, that all the nobility thereof brand their faces with a hot iron in token of honor.

He that boasts of sins never committed is a double devil. Some, who would sooner creep into a scabbard than draw a sword, boast of their robberies, to usurp the esteem of valor; whereas, first let them be well whipped for their lying, and as they like that, let them come afterward and entitle themselves to the gallows.

OF TRAVELLING.

IT is a good accomplishment to a man, if first the stock be well grown whereon travel is graffed, and these rules observed before, in, and after his going abroad.

Travel not too early, before thy judgment be risen; lest thou observest rather shows than substance, marking alone pageants, pictures, beautiful buildings, &c.

Get the language (in part), without which key thou shalt unlock little of moment. It is a great advantage to be one's own interpreter. Object not that the French tongue learnt in England must be unlearnt again in France; for it is easier to add than begin, and to pronounce than to speak.

Be well settled in thine own religion, lest, travelling out of England into Spain, thou goest out of God's blessing into the warm sun. They that go over maids for their religion, will be ravished at the sight of the first Popish church they enter into. But if first thou be well grounded, their fooleries shall rivet thy faith the faster, and travel shall give thee confirmation in that baptism thou didst receive at home.

Know most of the rooms of thy native country before thou goest over the threshold thereof; especially seeing England presents thee with so many observables. But late writers lack nothing but age, and home-wonders but distance to make them admired. 'T is a tale what Josephus writes of the two pillars set up by the sons of Seth in Syria, the one of brick, fire-proof, the other of stone, water-free, thereon engraving many heavenly matters to perpetuate learning in defiance of time. But it is truly moralized in our universities, Cambridge (of brick), and Oxford (of stone), wherein learning and religion are preserved, and where the worst college is more sightworthy than the best Dutch gymnasium. First view these, and the rest home-rarities; not like those English that can give a better account of Fontainebleau than Hampton Court, of the Spa than Bath, of Anas in Spain than Mole in Surrey.

Travel not beyond the Alps. Mr. Ascham did thank God that he was but nine days in Italy, wherein he saw in one city (Venice) more liberty to sin than in London he ever heard of in nine years. That some of our gentry have gone thither, and returned thence without infection, I more praise God's providence than their adventure.

To travel from the sun is uncomfortable. Yet the northern parts with much ice have some crystal, and want not their remarkables.

If thou wilt see much in a little, travel the Low Countries. Holland is all Europe in an Amsterdam print, for Minerva, Mars, and Mercury, learning, war, and traffic.

Be wise in choosing objects, diligent in marking, careful in remembering of them; yet herein men much follow their own humors. One asked a barber, who never before had been at the court, what he saw there. "Oh," said he, "the king was excellently well trimmed!"

Thus merchants most mark foreign havens, exchanges, and marts; soldiers note forts, armories, and magazines; scholars listen after libraries, disputations, and professors; statesmen observe courts of justice, councils, &c. Every one is partial in his own profession.

Labor to distil and unite into thyself the scattered perfections of several nations. But (as it was said of one who, with more industry than judgment, frequented a college library, and commonly made use of the worst notes he met with in any authors, that "he weeded the library") many weed foreign countries, bringing home Dutch drunkenness, Spanish pride, French wantonness, and Italian atheism. As for the good herbs, Dutch industry, Spanish loyalty, French courtesy, and Italian frugality, these they leave behind them. Others bring home just nothing; and because they singled not themselves from their countrymen, though some years beyond sea, were never out of England.

Continue correspondency with some choice foreign friend after thy return; as some professor or secretary, who virtually is the whole university, or State. 'T is but a dull Dutch fashion, their *album amicorum*, to make a dictionary of their friends' names; but a selected familiar in every country is useful; betwixt you there may be a letter-exchange. Be sure to return as good wares as thou receivest, and acquaint him with the remarkables of thy own country, and he will willingly continue the trade, finding it equally gainful.

Let discourse rather be easily drawn than willingly flow from thee, that thou mayst not seem weak to hold, or desirous to vent news, but content to gratify thy friends. Be sparing in reporting improbable truths, especially to the vulgar, who, instead of informing their judgments, will suspect thy credit. Disdain their peevish pride who rail on their native land (whose worse fault is that it bred such ungrateful fools), and in all their discourses prefer foreign countries, herein showing themselves of kin to the wild Irish, in loving their nurses better than their mothers.

OF COMPANY.

COMPANY is one of the greatest pleasures of the nature of man. For the beams of joy are made hotter by reflection when related to another; and otherwise gladness itself must grieve for want of one to express itself to.

It is unnatural for a man to court and hug solitariness. It is observed that the farthest islands in the world are so seated that there is none so remote but that from some shore of it another island or continent may be discerned; as if hereby nature invited countries to a mutual commerce one with another. Why, then, should any man affect to environ himself with so deep and great reservedness as not to communicate with the society of others? And though we pity those who made solitariness their refuge in time of persecution, we must condemn such as choose it in the Church's prosperity. For well may we count him not well in his wits who will live always under a bush because others in a storm shelter themselves under it.

Yet a desert is better than a debauched companion. For the wildness of the place is but uncheerful, whilst the wildness of bad persons is also infectious. Better, therefore, ride alone than have a thief's company. And such is a wicked man, who will rob thee of precious time, if he doth no more mischief. The Nazarites who might drink no wine, were also forbidden (*Num.* vi. 3) to eat grapes, whereof wine is made. We must not only avoid sin itself, but also the causes and occasions thereof; amongst which bad company (the limetwigs of the devil) is the chiefest, especially to catch those natures which, like the good-fellow planet Mercury, are most swayed by others.

If thou beest cast into bad company, like Hercules, thou must sleep with thy club in thine hand, and stand on thy guard. I mean, if against thy will the tempest of an unexpected occasion drives thee amongst such rocks; then be thou like the River Dee in Merionethshire in Wales, which, running through Pimble Meer, remains entire, and mingles not her streams with the waters of the lake. Though with them, be not of them; keep civil communion with them, but separate from their sins. And if against thy will thou fallest amongst wicked men, know to thy comfort thou art still in thy calling, and therefore in God's keeping, who, on thy prayers, will preserve thee.

The company he keeps is the comment by help whereof men expound the most close and mystical man, understanding him for one of the same religion, life, and manners with his associates. And though perchance he be not such a one, 't is just he should be counted so for conversing with them. Augustus Cæsar came thus to discern his two daughters' inclinations: for, being once at a public show, where much people was present, he observed that the grave senators talked with Livia, but loose youngsters and riotous persons with Julia.

"He that eats cherries with noblemen shall have his eyes spirted out with the stones." This outlandish proverb hath in it an English truth, that they who constantly converse with men far above their estates, shall reap shame and loss thereby. If thou payest nothing, they will count thee a sucker, no branch; a wen, no member of their company. If in payments thou keepest pace with them, their long strides will soon tire thy short legs. The beavers in New England, when some ten of them together draw a stick to the building of their lodging, set the weakest beavers to the lighter end of the log, and the strongest take the heaviest part thereof: whereas men often lay the greatest burden on the weakest back; and great persons, to teach meaner men to learn their distance, take pleasure to make them pay for their company. I except such men who, having some excellent quality, are gratis very welcome to their betters; such a one, though he pays not a penny of the shot, spends enough in lending them his time and discourse.

To affect always to be the best of the company, argues a base disposition. Gold always worn in the same purse with silver loses both of the color and weight; and so to converse always with inferiors degrades a man of his worth. Such there are that love to be the lords of the company, whilst the rest must be their tenants; as if bound by their lease to approve, praise, and admire whatsoever they say. These, knowing the lowness of their parts, love to live with dwarfs, that they may seem proper men. To come amongst their equals, they count it an abridgment of their freedom; but to be with their betters, they deem it flat slavery.

It is excellent for one to have a library of scholars, especially if they be plain to be read. I mean of a communicative nature, whose discourses are as full as fluent, and their judgments as right as their tongues ready: such men's talk shall be thy lectures. To conclude; good company is not only profitable whilst a man lives, but sometimes when he is dead. For he that was buried with the bones of Elisha, by a posthumous miracle of that prophet, recovered his life by lodging with such a grave-fellow.

OF APPAREL.

CLOTHES are for necessity; warm clothes for health; cleanly for decency; lasting for thrift; and rich for magnificence. Now there may be a fault in their number, if too various; making, if too vain; matter, if too costly; and mind of the wearer, if he takes pride therein. We come, therefore, to some general directions.

It 's a chargeable vanity to be constantly clothed above one's purse or place. I say constantly; for perchance sometimes it may be dispensed with. A great man, who himself was very plain in apparel, checked a gentleman for being over-fine; who modestly answered, "Your lordship hath better clothes at home, and I have worse." But, sure, no plea can be made when this luxury is grown to be ordinary. It was an arrogant act of Hubert, Archbishop of Canterbury, who, when King John had given his courtiers rich liveries, to ape the lion, gave his servants the like, wherewith the king was not a little offended. But what shall we say to the riot of our age, wherein (as peacocks are more gay than the eagle himself) subjects are grown braver than their sovereign?

'T is beneath a wise man always to wear clothes beneath men of his rank. True, there is a state sometimes in decent plainness. When a wealthy lord at a great solemnity had the plainest apparel, "Oh!" said one, "if you had marked it well, his suit had the richest pockets." Yet it argues no wisdom in clothes, always to stoop beneath his condition. When Antisthenes saw Socrates in a torn coat, he showed a hole thereof to the people: "And lo!" quoth he, "through this I see Socrates his pride."

He shows a light gravity who loves to be an exception from a general fashion. For the received custom in the place where we live is the most competent judge of decency; from which we must not appeal to our own opinion. When the French courtiers, mourning for their king, Henry the Second, had worn cloth a whole year, all silks became so vile in every man's eyes, that, if any was seen to wear them, he was presently accounted a mechanic or country fellow.

It 's a folly for one, Proteus-like, never to appear twice in one shape. Had some of our gallants been with the Israelites in the wilderness, when for forty years their clothes waxed not old, they would have been vexed, though their clothes were whole, to have been so long in one fashion. Yet, here I must confess, I understand not what is reported of Fulgentius, that he used the same garment winter and summer, and never altered his clothes, *etiam in sacris peragendis.*

He that is proud of the rustling of his silks, like a madman, laughs at the rattling of his fetters. For, indeed, clothes ought to be our remembrancers of our lost innocency. Besides, why should any brag of what 's but borrowed? Should the ostrich snatch off the gallant's feather, the beaver his hat, the goat his gloves, the sheep his suit, the silkworm his stockings, and neat his shoes, (to strip him no farther than modesty will give leave,) he would be left in a cold condition. And yet 't is more pardonable to be proud, even of cleanly rags, than (as many are) of affected slovenness. The one is proud of a molehill, the other of a dunghill.

To conclude; sumptuary laws in this land to reduce apparel to a set standard of price and fashion, according to the several states of men, have long been wished, but are little to be hoped for. Some think private men's superfluity is a necessary evil in a State, the floating of fashions affording a standing maintenance to many thousands which otherwise would be at a loss for a livelihood,—men maintaining more by their pride than by their charity.

OF BUILDING.

HE that alters an old house is tied as a translator to the original, and is confined to the fancy of the first builder. Such a man were unwise to pluck down good old buildings, to erect, perchance, worse new. But those that raise a new house from the ground are blameworthy if they make it not handsome, seeing to them method and confusion are both at a rate. In building we must respect situation, contrivance, receipt, strength, and beauty. Of situation —

Chiefly choose a wholesome air. For air is a dish one feeds on every minute, and, therefore, it need be good. Wherefore great men, (who may build where they please, as poor men where they can,) if herein they prefer their profit above their health, I refer them to their physicians to make them pay for it accordingly.

Wood and water are two staple commodities where they may be had. The former I confess hath made so much iron, that it must now be bought with the more silver, and grows daily dearer. But 't is as well pleasant as profitable to see a house cased with trees, like that of Anchises in Troy.

> "——— quanquam secreta parentis
> Anchisæ domus arboribusque obtecta recessit."

The worst is, where a place is bald of wood, no art can make it a periwig. As for water, begin with Pindar's beginning, ἄριστον μὲν ὕδωρ. The fort of Gogmagog Hills, nigh Cambridge, is counted impregnable but for want of water; the mischief of many houses, where servants must bring the well on their shoulders.

Next, a pleasant prospect is to be respected. A medley view (such as of water and land at Greenwich) best entertains the eyes, refreshing the wearied beholder with exchange of objects. Yet, I know a more profitable prospect, where the owner can only see his own land round about.

A fair entrance with an easy ascent gives a great grace to a building; where the hall is a preferment out of the court, the parlor out of the hall; not (as in some old buildings) where the doors are so low, pigmies must stoop, and the rooms so high that giants may stand upright. But now we are come to contrivance.

Let not thy common rooms be several, nor thy several rooms be common. The hall (which is a pandocheum) ought to lie open, and so ought passages and stairs (provided that the whole house be not spent in paths); chambers and closets are to be private and retired.

Light (God's eldest daughter) is a principal beauty in a building; yet it shines not alike from all parts of heaven. An east window welcomes the infant beams of the sun before they are of strength to do any harm, and is offensive to none but a sluggard. A south window in summer is a chimney with a fire in 't, and needs the screen of a curtain. In a west window, in summer time towards night, the sun grows low and over-familiar, with more light than delight. A north window is best for butteries and cellars, where the beer will be sour for the sun's smiling on it. Thorough-lights are best for rooms of entertainment, and windows on one side for dormitories. As for receipt: —

A house had better be too little for a day than too great for a year. And it 's easier borrowing of thy neighbor a brace of chambers for a night than a bag of money for a twelvemonth. It is vain, therefore, to proportion the receipt to an extraordinary occasion, as those who by overbuilding their houses have dilapidated their lands, and their states have been pressed to death under the weight of their house. As for strength: —

Country-houses must be substantives, able to stand of themselves; not like city buildings, supported by their neighbors on either side. By strength we mean such as may resist weather and time, not invasion, castles being out of date in this peaceable age. As for the making of moats round about, it is questionable whether the fogs be not more unhealthful than the fish bring profit, or the water defence. Beauty remains behind as the last to be regarded, because houses are made to be lived in, not looked on.

Let not the front look asquint on a stranger, but accost him right at his entrance. Uniformity also much pleaseth the eye; and 't is observed that freestone, like a fair complexion, soonest waxeth old, whilst brick keeps her beauty longest.

Let the office-houses observe the due distance from the mansion-house. Those are too familiar which presume to be of the same pile with it. The same may be said of stables and barns; without which a house is like a city without outworks, it can never hold out long.

Gardens also are to attend in their place. When God (*Genesis* ii. 9) planted a garden eastward, he made to grow out of the ground every tree pleasant to the sight, and good for food. Sure, he knew better what was proper to a garden than those who nowadays therein only feed the eyes and starve both taste and smell.

To conclude; in building, rather believe any man than an artificer in his own art for matter of charges, not that they cannot, but will not be faithful. Should they tell thee all the cost at the first, it would blast a young builder in the budding, and therefore they soothe thee up till it hath cost thee something to confute them. The spirit of building first possessed people after the flood, which then caused the confusion of languages, and since of the estate of many a man.

OF ANGER.

ANGER is one of the sinews of the soul: he that wants it hath a maimed mind, and with Jacob, sinew-shrunk in the hollow of his thigh, must needs halt. Nor is it good to converse with such as cannot be angry, and, with the Caspian Sea, never ebb nor flow. This anger is either heavenly, when one is offended for God; or hellish, when offended with God and goodness; or earthly, in temporal matters: which earthly anger (whereof we treat) may also be hellish, if for no cause, no great cause, too hot, or too long.

Be not angry with any without a cause. If thou beest, thou must not only, as the proverb saith, be appeased without amends, (having neither cost nor damage given thee,) but, as our Saviour saith, "be in danger of the judgment."

Be not mortally angry with any for a venial fault. He will make a strange combustion in the state of his soul, who, at the landing of every cockboat, sets the beacons on fire. To be angry for every toy debases the worth of thy anger; for he who will be angry for anything, will be angry for nothing.

Let not thy anger be so hot but that the most torrid zone thereof may be habitable.

Fright not people from thy presence with the terror of thy intolerable impatience. Some men, like a tiled house, are long before they take fire, but once on flame there is no coming near to quench them.

Take heed of doing irrevocable acts in thy passion; as the revealing of secrets, which makes thee a bankrupt for society ever after; neither do such things which once are done forever, so that no bemoaning can amend them. Samson's hair grew again, but not his eyes: time may restore some losses, others are never to be repaired. Wherefore in thy rage make no Persian decree, which cannot be reversed or repealed; but rather Polonian laws, which (they say) last but three days; do not in an instant what an age cannot recompense.

Anger kept till the next morning, with manna, doth putrefy and corrupt; save that manna corrupted not at all, and anger most of all, kept the next Sabbath. St. Paul saith, "Let not the sun go down on your wrath;" to carry news to the antipodes in another world of thy revengeful nature. Yet let us take the apostle's meaning rather than his words, with all possible speed to depose our passion, not understanding him so literally that we may take leave to be angry till sunset; then might our wrath lengthen with the days; and men in Greenland, where day lasts above a quarter of a year, have plentiful scope of revenge. And as the English (by command from William the Conqueror) always raked up their fire and put out their candles when the curfew-bell was rung, let us then also quench all sparks of anger and heat of passion.

He that keeps anger long in his bosom giveth place to the devil. And why should we make room for him, who will crowd in too fast of himself? Heat of passion makes our souls to chap, and the devil creeps in at the crannies. Yea, a furious man in his fits may seem possessed with a devil: foams, fumes, tears himself, is deaf and dumb in effect, to hear or speak reason; sometimes wallows, stares, stamps, with fiery eyes and flaming cheeks. Had Narcissus himself seen his own face when he had been angry, he could never have fallen in love with himself.

OF EXPECTING PREFERMENT.

THERE are as many several tenures of expectation as of possession; some nearer, some more remote; some grounded on strong, others on weaker reasons. (As for a groundless expectation, it is a wilful self-delusion.) We come to instructions how men should manage their hopes herein.

Hope not for impossibilities. For though the object of hope be *futurum possibile*, yet some are so mad as to feed their expectation on things, though not in themselves, yet to them impossible, if we consider the weakness of the means whereby they seek to attain them. He needs to stand on tiptoes that hopes to touch the moon; and those who expect what in reason they cannot expect, may expect.

Carefully survey what proportion the means thou hast bear to the end thou expectest. Count not a courtier's promise of course a specialty that he is bound to prefer thee. Seeing compliments oftentimes die in the speaking, why should thy hopes (grounded on them) live longer than the hearing? Perchance the text of his promise intended but common courtesies, which thy apprehension expounds speedy and special favors. Others make up the weakness of their means with conceit of the strength of their deserts, foolishly thinking that their own merits will be the undoubted patrons to present them to all void benefices.

The heir-apparent to the next preferment may be disinherited by an unexpected accident. A gentleman, servant to the Lord Admiral Howard, was suitor to a lady above his deserts, grounding the confidence of his success on his relation to so honorable a lord; which lord gave the anchor as badge of his office; and therefore this suitor wrote in a window, —

"If I be bold,
The anchor is my hold."

But his corrival to the same mistress, coming into the same room, wrote under, —

"Yet fear the worst:
What if the cable burst?"

Thus useless is the anchor of hope (good for nothing but to deceive those that rely on it), if the cable or small cords of means and causes whereon it depends fail and miscarry. Daily experience tenders too many examples. A gentleman who gave a basilisk for his arms or crest, promised to make a young kinsman of his his heir, which kinsman, to ingratiate himself, painted a basilisk in his study, and beneath it these verses: —

"Falleris aspectu basiliscum occidere, Plini,
Nam vitæ nostræ spem basiliscus alit."

"The basilisk 's the only stay
My life preserving still;
Pliny, thou li'dst when thou didst say
The basilisk doth kill."

But this rich gentleman dying, frustrated his expectation, and bequeathed all his estate to another; whereupon the epigram was thus altered: —

"Certe aluit, sed spe vana, spes vana venenum:
Ignoscas, Plini, verus es historicus."

"Indeed, vain hopes to me he gave,
Whence I my poison drew:
Pliny, thy pardon now I crave,
Thy writings are too true."

Proportion thy expenses to what thou hast in possession, not to thy expectancies. Otherwise, he that feeds on wind must needs be griped with the colic at last.

Imbrue not thy soul in bloody wishes of his death who parts thee and thy preferment, — a murder the more common because one cannot be arraigned for it on earth. But those are charitable murderers which wish them in heaven, not so much that they may have ease at their journey's end, but because they must needs take death in the way.

In earthly matters expectation takes up more joy on trust than the fruition of the thing is able to discharge. The lion is not so fierce as painted; nor are matters so fair as the pencil of the expectant limns them out in his hopes. They forecount their wives fair, fruitful, and rich, without any fault; their children witty, beautiful, and dutiful, without any frowardness: and as St. Basil held that roses in paradise, before man's fall, grew without prickles, they abstract the pleasures of things from the troubles annexed to them, which, when they come to enjoy, they must take both together.

When our hopes break, let our patience hold: relying on God's providence without murmuring, who often provides for men above what we can think or desire. When Robert Holgate could not peaceably enjoy his small living in Lincolnshire, because of the litigiousness of a neighboring knight, coming to London to right himself, he came into the favor of King Henry the Eighth, and got by degrees the archbishopric of York. Thus God sometimes defeats our hopes, or disturbs our possession of lesser favors, thereby to bestow on his servants better blessings, if not here, hereafter.

OF MEMORY.

IT is the treasure-house of the mind, wherein the monuments thereof are kept and preserved. Plato makes it the mother of the Muses; Aristotle sets it one degree further, making experience the mother of arts, memory the parent of experience. Philosophers place it in the rear of the head; and it seems the mine of memory lies there, because there naturally men dig for it, scratching it when they are at a loss. This again is twofold: one, the simple retention of things; the other, a regaining them when forgotten.

Brute creatures equal, if not exceed, men in a bare retentive memory. Through how many labyrinths of woods, without other clue of thread than natural instinct, doth the hunted hare return to her muce! How doth the little bee, flying into several meadows and gardens, sipping of many cups, yet never intoxicated, through an ocean (as I may say) of air, steadily steer herself home, without help of card or compass! But these cannot play an after-game, and recover what they have forgotten, which is done by the meditation of discourse.

Artificial memory is rather a trick than an art, and more for the gain of the teacher than profit of the learners; like the tossing of a pike, which is no part of the postures and motions thereof, and is rather for ostentation than use, to show the strength and nimbleness of the arm, and is often used by wandering soldiers as an introduction to beg. Understand it of the artificial rules which at this day are delivered by memory-mountebanks; for, sure, an art thereof may be made (wherein as yet the world is defective), and that no more destructive to natural memory than spectacles are to eyes, which girls in Holland wear from twelve years of age. But till this be found out, let us observe these plain rules: —

First, soundly infix in thy mind what thou desirest to remember. What wonder is it if agitation of business jog that out of thy head which was there rather tacked than fastened? Whereas those notions which get in by *violenta possessio*, will abide there till *ejectio firma*, sickness or extreme age, dispossess them. It is best knocking in the nail overnight, and clinching it the next morning.

Overburden not thy memory to make so faithful a servant a slave. Remember Atlas was weary. Have as much reason as a camel to rise when thou hast thy full load. Memory, like a purse, if it be over-full that it cannot shut, all will drop out of it. Take heed of a gluttonous curiosity to feed on many things, lest the greediness of the appetite of thy memory spoil the digestion thereof. Beza's case was peculiar and memorable: being above fourscore years of age, he perfectly could say by heart any Greek chapter in St. Paul's epistles, or anything else which he had learnt long before, but forgot whatsoever was newly told him; his memory, like an inn, retaining old guests, but having no room to entertain new.

Spoil not thy memory with thine own jealousy, nor make it bad by suspecting it. How canst thou find that true which thou wilt not trust? St. Augustine tells us of his friend Simplicius, who, being asked, could tell all Virgil's verses backward and forward, and yet the same party vowed to God that he knew not that he could do it till they did try him. Sure, there is concealed strength in men's memories, which they take no notice of.

Marshal thy notions into a handsome method. One will carry twice more weight, trussed and packed up in bundles, than when it lies untowardly flapping and hanging about his shoulders. Things orderly fardled up under heads are most portable.

Adventure not all thy learning in one bottom, but divide it betwixt thy memory and thy note-books. He that with Bias carries all his learning about him in his head will utterly be beggared and bankrupt if a violent disease, a merciless thief, should rob and strip him. I know some have a commonplace against commonplace books, and yet, perchance, will privately make use of what publicly they declaim against. A commonplace book contains many notions in garrison, whence the owner may draw out an army into the field on competent warning.

Moderate diet and good air preserve memory; but what air is best I dare not define, when such great ones differ. Some say a pure and subtle air is best, another commends a thick and foggy air. For the Pisans, sited in the fens and marshes of Arnus, have excellent memories, as if the foggy air were a cap for their heads.

Thankfulness to God for it continues the memory; whereas some proud people have been visited with such oblivion that they have forgotten their own names. Staupitius, tutor to Luther, and a godly man, in a vain ostentation of his memory, repeated Christ's genealogy (*Matt.* i.) by heart in his sermon, but being out about the captivity of Babylon, "I see," saith he, "God resisteth the proud," and so betook himself to his book.

Abuse not thy memory to be sin's register, nor make advantage thereof for wickedness. Excellently Augustine,—*Quidam vero pessimi memoriâ sunt mirabili, qui tanto pejores sunt, quanto minus possunt, quæ male cogitant, oblivisci.*

OF FANCY.

IT is an inward sense of the soul for a while retaining and examining things brought in thither by the common sense. It is the most boundless and restless faculty of the soul; for whilst the understanding and the will are kept as it were *in libera custodia* to their objects of *verum* and *bonum*, the fancy is free from all engagements. It digs without spade, sails without ship, flies without wings, builds without charges, fights without bloodshed, in a moment striding from the centre to the circumference of the world, by a kind of omnipotency creating and annihilating things in an instant; and things divorced in nature are married in fancy, as in a lawful place. It is also most restless; whilst the senses are bound, and reason in a manner asleep, fancy, like a sentinel, walks the round, ever working, never wearied. The chief diseases of the fancy are, either that they are too wild and high-soaring, or else too low and grovelling, or else too desultory and overvoluble. Of the first: —

If thy fancy be but a little too rank, age itself will correct it. To lift too high is no fault in a young horse, because with travelling he will mend it for his own ease. Thus lofty fancies in young men will come down of themselves, and in process of time the overplus will shrink to be but even measure. But if this will not do it, then observe these rules.

Take part always with thy judgment against thy fancy in anything wherein they shall dissent. If thou suspectest thy conceits too luxuriant, herein account thy suspicion a legal conviction, and damn whatsoever thou doubtest of. Warily Tully,—*Bene monent, qui vetant quicquam facere, de quo dubitas, æquum sit an iniquum.*

Take the advice of a faithful friend, and submit thy inventions to his censure. When thou pennest an oration, let him have the power of *index expurgatorius*, to expunge what he pleaseth; and do not thou like a fond mother cry if the child of thy brain be corrected for playing the wanton. Mark the arguments and reasons of his alterations, why that phrase least proper, this passage more cautious and advised, and after a while thou shalt perform the place in thine own person, and not go out of thyself for a censurer. If thy fancy be too low and humble,

Let thy judgment be king but not tyrant over it, to condemn harmless, yea, commendable conceits. Some, for fear their orations should giggle, will not let them smile. Give it also liberty to rove, for it will not be extravagant. There is no danger that weak folks if they walk abroad will straggle far, as wanting strength.

Acquaint thyself with reading poets, for there fancy is in her throne; and in time the sparks of the author's wit will catch hold on the reader and inflame him with love, liking, and desire of imitation. I confess there is more required to teach one to write than to see a copy; however, there is a secret force of fascination in reading poems to raise and provoke fancy. If thy fancy be over-voluble, then

Whip this vagrant home to the first object whereon it should be settled. Indeed, nimbleness is the perfection of this faculty, but levity the bane of it. Great is the difference betwixt a swift horse and a skittish, that will stand on no ground. Such is the ubiquitary fancy, which will keep long residence on no one subject, but is so courteous to strangers that it ever welcomes that conceit most which comes last; and new species supplant the old ones before seriously considered. If this be the fault of thy fancy, I say whip it home to the first object whereon it should be settled. This do as often as occasion requires, and by degrees the fugitive servant will learn to abide by his work without running away.

Acquaint thyself by degrees with hard and knotty studies, as school-divinity, which will clog thy over-nimble fancy. True, at the first it will be as welcome to thee as a prison, and their very solutions will seem knots unto thee. But take not too much at once, lest thy brain turn edge. Taste it first as a potion for physic, and by degrees thou shalt drink it as beer for thirst: practice will make it pleasant. Mathematics are also good for this purpose: if beginning to try a conclusion, thou must make an end, lest thou losest thy pains that are past, and must proceed seriously and exactly. I meddle not with those bedlam fancies, all whose conceits are antiques, but leave them for the physician to purge with hellebore.

To clothe low-creeping matter with high-flown language is not fine fancy, but flat foolery. It rather loads than raises a wren to fasten the feathers of an ostrich to her wings. Some men's speeches are like the high mountains in Ireland, having a dirty bog in the top of them; the very ridge of them in high words having nothing of worth, but what rather stalls than delights the auditor.

Fine fancies in manufactures invent engines rather pretty than useful; and commonly one trade is too narrow for them. They are better to project new ways than to prosecute old, and are rather skilful in many mysteries than thriving in one. They affect not voluminous inventions, wherein many years must constantly be spent to perfect them, except there be in them variety of pleasant employment.

Imagination, the work of the fancy, hath produced real effects. Many serious and sad examples hereof may be produced: I will only insist on a merry one. A gentleman having led a company of children beyond their usual journey, they began to be weary, and jointly cried to him to carry them; which, because of their multitude, he could not do, but told them he would provide them horses to ride on. Then cutting little wands out of the hedge as nags for them, and a great stake as a gelding for himself, thus mounted, fancy put mettle into their legs, and they came cheerfully home.

Fancy runs most furiously when a guilty conscience drives it. One that owed much money, and had many creditors, as he walked London streets in the evening, a tenter-hook catched his cloak. "At whose suit?" said he, conceiving some bailiff had arrested him. Thus guilty consciences are afraid where no fear is, and count every creature they meet a sergeant sent from God to punish them.

OF NATURAL FOOLS.

THEY have the cases of men, and little else of them besides speech and laughter. And indeed it may seem strange, that, *risibile* being the property of man alone, they who have least of man should have most thereof, laughing without cause or measure.

Generally, nature hangs out a sign of simplicity in the face of a fool; and there is enough in his countenance for a hue and cry to take him on suspicion: or else it is stamped on the figure of his body; their heads sometimes so little that there is no room for wit; sometimes so long that there is no wit for so much room.

Yet some by their faces may pass current enough till they cry themselves down by their speaking. Thus men know the bell is cracked when they hear it tolled; yet some that have stood out the assault of two or three questions, and have answered pretty rationally, have afterwards, of their own accord, betrayed and yielded themselves to be fools.

The oaths and railing of fools is oftentimes no fault of theirs but their teachers. The Hebrew word *barak* signifies to bless, and to curse; and 't is the speaker's pleasure if he use it in the worst acceptation. Fools of themselves are equally capable to pray and to swear; they, therefore, have the greatest sin who by their example or otherwise teach them so to do.

One may get wisdom by looking on a fool. In beholding him, think how much thou art beholden to him that suffered thee not to be like him: only God's pleasure put a difference betwixt you. And consider that a fool and a wise man are alike both in the starting-place, their birth, and at the post, their death; only they differ in the race of their lives.

It is unnatural to laugh at a natural. How can the object of thy pity be the subject of thy pastime? I confess sometimes the strangeness, and, as I may say, witty simplicity of their actions may extort a smile from a serious man, who at the same time may smile at them and sorrow for them. But it is one thing to laugh at them *in transitu*, a snap and away, and another to make a set meal in jeering them, and as the Philistines, to send for Samson to make them sport.

To make a trade of laughing at a fool is the highway to become one. Tully confesseth that whilst he laughed at one Hircus, a very ridiculous man, *dum illum rideo pene factus sum ille:* and one telleth us of Gallus Vibius, a man first of great eloquence, and afterwards of great madness, which seized not on him so much by accident as his own affectation, so long mimically imitating madmen that he became one.

Many have been the wise speeches of fools, though not so many as the foolish speeches of wise men. Now the wise speeches of these silly souls proceed from one of these reasons: either because talking much and shooting often they must needs hit the mark sometimes, though not by aim, by hap; or else, because a fool's *mediocriter* is *optime*, sense from his mouth, a sentence, and a tolerable speech cried up for an apothegm; or, lastly, because God may sometimes illuminate them, and, especially towards their death, admit them to the possession of some part of reason. A poor beggar in Paris, being very hungry, stayed so long in a cook's shop, who was dishing up of meat, till his stomach was satisfied with the only smell thereof. The choleric covetous cook demanded of him to pay for his breakfast. The poor man denied it, and the controversy was referred to the deciding of the next man that should pass by, which chanced to be the most notorious idiot in the whole city. He, on the relation of the matter, determined that the poor man's money should be put betwixt two empty dishes, and the cook should be recompensed with the jingling of the poor man's money, as he was satisfied with the only smell of the cook's meat. And this is affirmed by credible writers as no fable, but an undoubted fact. More waggish was that of a rich landed fool, whom a courtier had begged, and carried about to wait on him. He, coming with his master to a gentleman's house where the picture of a fool was wrought in a fair suit of arras, cut the picture out with a penknife. And being chidden for so doing, "You have more cause," said he, "to thank me; for if my master had seen the picture of the fool, he would have begged the hangings of the king, as he did my lands." When the standers-by comforted a natural which lay on his death-bed, and told him that four proper fellows should carry his body to the church: "Yea," quoth he, "but I had rather by half go thither myself;" and then prayed to God at his last gasp not to require more of him than he gave him.

As for a changeling, which is not one child changed for another, but one child on a sudden much changed from itself; and for a jester, which some count a necessary evil in a court, an office which none but he that hath wit can perform, and none but he that wants wit will perform, I conceive them not to belong to the present subject.

OF RECREATIONS.

RECREATION is a second creation, when weariness hath almost annihilated one's spirits. It is the breathing of the soul, which otherwise would be stifled with continual business. We may trespass in them, if using such as are forbidden by the lawyer as against the statutes; physician, as against health; divine, as against conscience.

Be well satisfied in thy conscience of the lawfulness of the recreation thou usest. Some fight against cock-fighting, and bait bull and bear-baiting, because man is not to be a common barrator to set the creatures at discord; and seeing antipathy betwixt creatures was kindled by man's sin, what pleasure can he take to see it burn? Others are of the contrary opinion, and that Christianity gives us a placard to use these sports; and that man's charter of dominion over the creatures enables him to employ them as well for pleasure as necessity. In these, as in all other doubtful recreations, be well assured first of the legality of them. He that sins against his conscience, sins with a witness.

Spill not the morning (the quintessence of the day) in recreations. For sleep itself is a recreation; add not therefore sauce to sauce; and he cannot properly have any title to be refreshed who was not first faint. Pastime, like wine, is poison in the morning. It is then good husbandry to sow the head, which hath lain fallow all night, with some serious work. Chiefly, intrench not on the Lord's day, to use unlawful sports; this were to spare thine own flock, and to shear God's lamb.

Let thy recreations be ingenious, and bear proportion with thine age. If thou sayest with Paul, "When I was a child I did as a child," say also with him, "But when I was a man I put away childish things." Wear also the child's coat, if thou usest his sports.

Take heed of boisterous and over-violent exercises. Ringing oftentimes hath made good music on the bells, and put men's bodies out of tune, so that by overheating themselves they have rung their own passing-bell.

Yet the ruder sort of people scarce count anything a sport which is not loud and violent. The Muscovite women esteem none loving husbands except they beat their wives. 'T is no pastime with country clowns that cracks not pates, breaks not shins, bruises not limbs, tumbles and tosses not all the body. They think themselves not warm in their gears till they are all on fire; and count it but dry sport till they swim in their own sweat. Yet I conceive the physicians' rule in exercises, *ad ruborem* but *non ad sudorem*, is too scant measure.

Refresh that part of thyself which is most wearied. If thy life be sedentary, exercise thy body; if stirring and active, recreate thy mind. But take heed of cozening thy mind, in setting it to do a double task under pretence of giving it a play-day, as in the labyrinth of chess, and other tedious and studious games.

Yet recreations distasteful to some dispositions relish best to others. Fishing with an angle is to some rather a torture than a pleasure, to stand an hour as mute as the fish they mean to take: yet herewithal Doctor Whitaker was much delighted. When some noblemen had gotten William Cecil, Lord Burleigh and Treasurer of England, to ride with them a-hunting, and the sport began to be cold, "What call you this?" said the Treasurer. "Oh now," said they, "the dogs are at a fault." "Yea," quoth the Treasurer, "take me again in such a fault, and I 'll give you leave to punish me." Thus as soon may the same meat please all palates as the same sport suit with all dispositions.

Running, leaping, and dancing, the descants on the plain song of walking, are all excellent exercises. And yet those are the best recreations which, besides refreshing, enable, at least dispose, men to some other good ends. Bowling teaches men's hands and eyes mathematics and the rules of proportion; swimming hath saved many a man's life, when himself hath been both the wares and the ship; tilting and fencing is war without anger; and manly sports are the grammar of military performance.

But, above all, shooting is a noble recreation, and a half liberal art. A rich man told a poor man that he walked to get a stomach for his meat: "And I," said the poor man, "walk to get meat for my stomach." Now shooting would have fitted both their turns; it provides food when men are hungry, and helps digestion when they are full. King Edward the Sixth, though he drew no strong bow, shot very well; and when once John Dudley, Duke of Northumberland, commended him for hitting the mark, "You shot better," quoth the King, "when you shot off my good uncle Protector's head."

Some sports being granted to be lawful, more propend to be ill than well used. Such I count stage-plays, when made always the actor's work, and often the spectator's recreation. Zeuxis, the curious picturer, painted a boy holding a dishful of grapes in his hand, done so lively that the birds being deceived flew to peck the grapes. But Zeuxis, in an ingenious choler, was angry with his own workmanship. "Had I," said he, "made the boy as lively as the grapes, the birds would have been afraid to touch them." Thus two things are set forth to us in stage-plays: some grave sentences, prudent counsels, and punishment of vicious examples; and with these, desperate oaths, lustful talk, and riotous acts are so personated to the life, that wantons are tickled with delight, and feed their palates upon them. It seems the goodness is not portrayed out with equal accents of liveliness as the wicked things are; otherwise men would be deterred from vicious courses, with seeing the woful success which follows them. But the main is, wanton speeches on stages are the devil's ordinance to beget badness; but I question whether the pious speeches spoken there be God's ordinance to increase goodness, as wanting both his institution and benediction.

Choke not thy soul with immoderate pouring in the cordial of pleasures. The creation lasted but six days of the first week: profane they whose recreation lasts seven days every week. Rather abridge thyself of thy lawful liberty herein; it being a wary rule which St. Gregory gives us,—*Solus in illicitis non cadit, qui se aliquando et a licitis caute restringit.* And then recreations shall both strengthen labor and sweeten rest, and we may expect God's blessing and protection on us in following them, as well as in doing our work; for he that saith grace for his meat, in it prays also to God to bless the sauce unto him. As for those that will not take lawful pleasure, I am afraid they will take unlawful pleasure, and by lacing themselves too hard grow awry on one side.

OF TOMBS

TOMBS are the clothes of the dead: a grave is but a plain suit, and a rich monument is one embroidered. Most moderate men have been careful for the decent interment of their corpses. Few of the fond mind of Arbogastus, an Irish saint, and bishop of Spires in Germany, who would be buried near the gallows, in imitation of our Saviour, whose grave was in Mount Calvary near the place of execution.

'T is a provident way to make one's tomb in

one's lifetime; both hereby to prevent the negligence of heirs, and to mind him of his mortality. Virgil tells us that when bees swarm in the air, and two armies, meeting together, fight as it were a set battle with great violence, cast but a little dust upon them and they will be quiet, —

> "Hi motus animorum, atque hæc certamina tanta
> Pulveris exigui jactu compressa quiescunt."

> "These stirrings of their minds and strivings vast,
> If but a little dust on them be cast,
> Are straightways stinted, and quite overpast."

Thus the most ambitious motions and thoughts of man's mind are quickly quelled when dust is thrown on him, whereof his fore-prepared sepulchre is an excellent remembrancer.

Yet some seem to have built their tombs, therein to bury their thoughts of dying, never thinking thereof, but embracing the world with greater greediness. A gentleman made choice of a fair stone, and intending the same for his grave-stone, caused it to be pitched up in a field a pretty distance from his house, and used often to shoot at it for his exercise. "Yea, but," said a wag that stood by, "you would be loath, sir, to hit the mark;" and so are many unwilling to die, who, notwithstanding, have erected their monuments.

Tombs ought in some sort to be proportioned

not to the wealth, but deserts of the party interred. Yet may we see some rich man of mean worth loaden under a tomb big enough for a prince to bear. There were officers appointed in the Grecian games, who always, by public authority, did pluck down the statues erected to the victors, if they exceeded the true symmetry and proportion of their bodies. We need such nowadays to order monuments to men's merits, chiefly to reform such depopulating tombs as have no good fellowship with them, but engross all the room, leaving neither seats for the living nor graves for the dead. It was a wise and thrifty law which Reutha, King of Scotland, made, that noblemen should have so many pillars, or long pointed stones, set on their sepulchres as they had slain enemies in the wars. If this order were also enlarged to those who in peace had excellently deserved of the Church or commonwealth, it might well be revived.

Over-costly tombs are only baits for sacrilege. Thus sacrilege hath beheaded that peerless prince, King Henry the Fifth, the body of whose statue on his tomb in Westminster was covered over with silver plate gilded, and his head of massy silver; both which now are stolen away: yea, hungry palates will feed on coarser meat. I had rather Mr. Stow,* than

* In the *Description of London.*

I, should tell you of a nobleman who sold the monuments of noblemen, in St. Augustine's Church in Broad Street, for an hundred pounds, which cost many thousands, and in the place thereof made fair stabling for horses; as if Christ, who was born in a stable, should be brought into it the second time. It was not without cause in the civil law that a wife might be divorced from her husband, if she could prove him to be one that had broken the sepulchres of the dead: for it was presumed he must needs be a tyrannical husband to his wife, who had not so much mercy as to spare the ashes of the departed.

The shortest, plainest, and truest epitaphs are best. I say, the shortest; for when a passenger sees a chronicle written on a tomb, he takes it on trust some great man lies there buried, without taking pains to examine who he is. Mr. Cambden, in his "Remains," presents us with examples of great men that had little epitaphs. And when once I asked a witty gentleman, an honored friend of mine, what epitaph was fittest to be written on Mr. Cambden's tomb, "Let it be," said he, "CAMBDEN'S REMAINS."

I say also the plainest; for except the sense lie above-ground, few will trouble themselves to dig for 't. Lastly, it must be true: not as in some monuments, where the red veins in the marble may seem to blush at the falsehoods written on it. He was a witty man that first taught a stone to speak, but he was a wicked man that taught it first to lie.

A good memory is the best monument. Others are subject to casualty and time, and we know that the pyramids themselves, doting with age, have forgotten the names of their founders. To conclude, let us be careful to provide rest for our souls, and our bodies will provide rest for themselves. And let us not be herein like unto gentlewomen, which care not to keep the inside of the orange, but candy and preserve only the outside thereof.

OF DEFORMITY.

DEFORMITY is either natural, voluntary, or adventitious, being either caused by God's unseen providence (by men nicknamed chance) or by man's cruelty. We will take them in order.

If thou beest not so handsome as thou wouldst have been, thank God thou art no more unhandsome than thou art. 'T is his mercy thou art not the mark for passengers' fingers to point at, an heteroclite in nature, with some member defective or redundant.

Be glad that thy clay cottage hath all the necessary rooms thereto belonging, though the outside be not so fairly plastered as some others.

Yet is it lawful and commendable by art to correct the defects and deformities of nature. Ericthonius being a goodly man from the girdle upwards, but, as the poets feign, having downwards the body of a serpent (moralize him to have had some defect in his feet), first invented chariots, wherein he so sat that the upper parts of him might be seen, and the rest of his body concealed. Little heed is to be given to his lying pen, who maketh Anna Bollen, mother to Queen Elizabeth, the first finder-out and wearer of ruffs, to cover a wen she had in her neck. Yet the matter 's not much; such an addition of art being without any fraud or deceit.

Mock not at those who are misshapen by nature. There is the same reason of the poor and of the deformed; he that despiseth them, despiseth God that made them. A poor man is a picture of God's own making, but set in a plain frame, not gilded; a deformed man is also his workmanship, but not drawn with even lines and lively colors: the former, not for want of wealth, as the latter not for want of skill, but both for the pleasure of the maker. As for Aristotle, who would have parents expose their deformed children to the wide world without caring for them, his opinion herein, not only deformed but most monstrous, deserves rather to be exposed to the scorn and contempt of all men.

Some people, handsome by nature, have wilfully deformed themselves; such as wear Bacchus his colors in their faces, arising not from having, but being, bad livers. When the woman (1 *Kings*, iii. 21) considered the child that was laid by her, "Behold," said she, "it was not my son which I did bear." Should God survey the faces of many men and women, he would not own and acknowledge them for those which he created, many are so altered in color, and some in sex, women to men, and men to women, in their monstrous fashions, so that they who behold them cannot by the evidence of their apparel give up their verdict of what sex they are.

Confessors which wear the badges of truth are thereby made the more beautiful, though deformed in time of persecution for Christ's sake through men's malice. This made Constantine the Great to kiss the hole in the face of Paphnutius, out of which the tyrant Maximinus had bored his eye for the profession of the faith, the good emperor making much of the socket even when the candle was put out. Next these, wounds in war are most honorable: halting is the stateliest march of a soldier; and 't is a brave sight to see the flesh of an ancient as torn as his colors. He that mocks at the marks of valor in a soldier's face, is likely to live to have the brands of justice on his own shoulders.

Nature oftentimes recompenseth deformed bodies with excellent wits. Witness Æsop, than whose fables children cannot read an easier, nor men a wiser book; for all latter moralists do but write comments upon them. Many jeering wits, who have thought to have rid at their ease on the bowed backs of some cripples, have by their unhappy answers been unhorsed and thrown flat on their own backs. A jeering gentleman commended a beggar, who was deformed and little better than blind, for having an excellent eye. "True," said the beggar, "for I can discern an honest man from such a knave as you are."

Their souls have been the chapels of sanctity, whose bodies have been the 'spitals of deformity. An emperor of Germany, coming by chance on a Sunday into a church, found there a most misshaped priest, *pene portentum naturæ*, insomuch as the emperor scorned and contemned him. But when he heard him read those words in the service, "for it is he that made us, and not we ourselves," the emperor checked his own proud thoughts, and made inquiry into the quality and condition of the man, and finding him on examination to be most learned and devout, he made him Archbishop of Colen, which place he did excellently discharge.

OF PLANTATIONS.

PLANTATIONS make mankind broader, as generation makes it thicker. To advance a happy plantation, the undertakers, planters, and place itself, must contribute their endeavors.

Let the prime undertakers be men of no shallow heads, nor narrow fortunes; such as have a real estate, so that, if defeated in their adventure abroad, they may have a retreating place at home, and such as will be contented with their present loss to be benefactors to posterity. But if the prince himself be pleased not only to wink at them with his permission, but also to smile on them with his encouragement, there is great hope of success; for then he will grant them some immunities and privileges. Otherwise (infants must be swathed, not laced) young plantations will never grow, if straitened with as hard laws as settled commonwealths.

Let the planters be honest, skilful, and painful people. For if they be such as leap thither from the gallows, can any hope for cream out of scum? when men send (as I may say) Christian savages to heathen savages. It was rather bitterly than falsely spoken concerning one of our western plantations (consisting most of dissolute people), "that it was very like unto England, as being spit out of the very mouth of it." Nor must the planters be only honest, but industrious also. What hope is there that they who were drones at home will be bees abroad, especially if far off from any to oversee them?

Let the place be naturally strong, or at leastwise capable of fortification. For though, at the first, planters are sufficiently fenced with their own poverty, and though at the beginning their worst enemies will spare them out of pity to themselves, their spoil not countervailing the cost of spoiling them, yet, when once they have gotten wealth, they must get strength to defend it. Here, know, islands are easily shut, whereas continents have their doors ever open, not to be bolted without great charges. Besides, unadvised are those planters who, having choice of ground, have built their towns in places of a servile nature, as being overawed and constantly commanded by some hills about them.

Let it have a self-sufficiency, or some staple

commodity to balance traffic with other countries. As for a self-sufficiency, few countries can stand alone, and such as can for matter of want, will for wantonness lean on others. Staple commodities are such as are never out of fashion, as belonging to a man's being, — being with comfort, being with delight, the luxury of our age having made superfluities necessary. And such a place will thrive the better when men may say with Isaac, "Rehoboth, now the Lord hath made room for us," when new colonies come not in with extirpation of the natives; for this is rather a supplanting than a planting.

Let the planters labor to be loved and feared of the natives; with whom let them use all just bargaining, being as naked in their dealings with them as the other in their going, keeping all covenants, performing all promises with them. Let them embrace all occasions to convert them, knowing that each convert is a conquest; and it is more honor to overcome paganism in one than to conquer a thousand pagans. As for the inscription of a deity in their hearts, it need not be new written, but only new scoured in them. I am confident that America (though the youngest sister of the four) is now grown marriageable, and daily hopes to get Christ to her husband by the preaching of the gospel. This makes me attentively to listen after some Protestant first-fruits, in hope the harvest will ripen afterwards.

OF CONTENTMENT.

IT is one property which (they say) is required of those who seek for the philosopher's stone, that they must not do it with any covetous desire to be rich; for otherwise they shall never find it. But most true it is that whosoever would have this jewel of contentment (which turns all into gold, yea, want into wealth) must come with minds divested of all ambitious and covetous thoughts; else are they never likely to obtain it. We will describe contentment first negatively.

It is not a senseless stupidity what becomes of our outward estates. God would have us take notice of all accidents which from him happen to us in worldly matters. Had the martyrs had the dead palsy before they went to the stake to be burnt, their sufferings had not been so glorious.

It is not a word-braving, or scorning of all wealth in discourse. Generally, those who boast most of contentment have least of it. Their very boasting shows that they want something, and basely beg it, namely, commendation. These, in their language, are like unto kites in their flying, which mount in the air so scornfully as if they disdained to stoop for the whole earth, fetching about many stately circuits: but what is the spirit these conjurers with so many circles intend to raise? A poor chicken, or perchance a piece of carrion: and so the height of the others' proud boasting will humble itself for a little base gain.

But it is an humble and willing submitting ourselves to God's pleasure in all conditions. One observeth (how truly I dispute not) that the French naturally have so elegant and graceful a carriage, that, what posture of body soever in their salutations, or what fashion of attire soever they are pleased to take on them, it doth so beseem them that one would think nothing can become them better. Thus contentment makes men carry themselves gracefully in wealth, want, in health, sickness, freedom, fetters, yea, what condition soever God allots them.

It is no breach of contentment for men to complain that their sufferings are unjust, as offered by men; provided they allow them for just, as proceeding from God, who useth wicked men's injustice to correct his children. But let us take heed that we bite not so high at the handle of the rod as to fasten on his hand that holds it; our discontentments mounting so high as to quarrel with God himself.

It is no breach of contentment for men by lawful means to seek the removal of their misery and bettering of their estate. Thus men ought by industry to endeavor the getting of more wealth, ever submitting themselves to God's will. A lazy hand is no argument of a contented heart. Indeed, he that is idle, and followeth after vain persons, shall have enough; but how? (*Prov.* xxviii. 19,) "shall have poverty enough."

God's spirit is the best schoolmaster to teach contentment, — a schoolmaster who can make good scholars, and warrant the success as well as his endeavor. The school of sanctified afflictions is the best place to learn contentment in: I say, sanctified; for naturally, like resty horses, we go the worse for the beating, if God bless not afflictions unto us.

Contentment consisteth not in adding more fuel, but in taking away some fire; not in multiplying of wealth, but in subtracting men's desires. Worldly riches, like nuts, tear many clothes in getting them, spoil many teeth in cracking them, but fill no belly with eating them, obstructing only the stomach with toughness, and filling the bowels with windiness; yea, our souls may sooner surfeit than be satisfied with earthly things. He that at first thought ten thousand pounds too much for any one man, will afterwards think ten millions too little for himself.

Men create more discontents to themselves than ever happened to them for others. We read of our Saviour, that, at the burial of Lazarus, (*John* xi. 33,) ἐτάραξεν ἑαυτόν, "he troubled himself," by his spirit raising his own passions, though without any ataxy or sinful disturbance. What was an act of power in him is an act of weakness in other men: man disquieteth himself in vain with many causeless and needless afflictions.

Pious meditations much advantage contentment in adversity. Such as these are: to consider, first, that more are beneath us than above us; secondly, many of God's dear saints have been in the same condition; thirdly, we want rather superfluities than necessities; fourthly, the more we have, the more we must account for; fifthly, earthly blessings, through man's corruption, are more prone to be abused than well used; sixthly, we must leave all earthly wealth at our death, "and riches avail not in the day of wrath:" but, as some use to fill up the stamp of light gold with dirt, thereby to make it weigh the heavier, so it seems some men load their souls with thick clay, to make them pass the better in God's balance, but all to no purpose; seventhly, the less we have, the less it will grieve us to leave this world; lastly, it is the will of God, and therefore both for his glory and our good, whereof we ought to be assured. I have heard how a gentleman, travelling in a misty morning, asked of a shepherd (such men being generally skilled in the physiognomy of the heavens) what weather it would be. "It will be," said the shepherd, "what weather shall please me:" and being courteously requested to express his meaning, "Sir," saith he, "it shall be what weather pleaseth God, and what weather pleaseth God pleaseth me." Thus contentment maketh men to have even what they think fitting themselves, because submitting to God's will and pleasure.

To conclude: a man ought to be like unto a cunning actor, who, if he be enjoined to represent the person of some prince or nobleman, does it with a grace and comeliness; if by and by he be commanded to lay that aside and play the beggar, he does that as willingly and as well. But, as it happened in a tragedy (to spare naming the person and place), that one, being to act Theseus, in "Hercules Furens," coming out of hell, could not for a long time be persuaded to wear old sooty clothes proper to his part, but would needs come out of hell in a white satin doublet, so we are generally loath, and it goes against flesh and blood to live in a low and poor estate, but would fain act in richer and handsomer clothes, till grace, with much ado, subdues our rebellious stomachs to God's will.

OF BOOKS.

SOLOMON saith truly, "Of making many books there is no end;" so insatiable is the thirst of men therein: as also endless is the desire of many in buying and reading them. But we come to our rules.

It is a vanity to persuade the world one hath much learning by getting a great library. As soon shall I believe every one is valiant that hath a well-furnished armory. I guess good housekeeping by the smoking, not the number of the tunnels, as knowing that many of them (built merely for uniformity) are without chimneys, and more without fires. Once a dunce, void of learning but full of books, flouted a library-less scholar with these words, — *Salve, doctor sine libris:* but the next day the scholar coming into this jeerer's study crowded with books, — *Salvete, libri,* saith he, *sine doctore.*

Few books well selected are best. Yet, as a certain fool bought all the pictures that came out, because he might have his choice; such is the vain humor of many men in gathering of books: yet when they have done all, they miss their end, it being in the editions of authors as in the fashions of clothes, when a man thinks he hath gotten the latest and newest, presently another newer comes out.

Some books are only cursorily to be tasted of. Namely, first, voluminous books, the task of a man's life to read them over; secondly, auxiliary books, only to be repaired to on occasions; thirdly, such as are mere pieces of formality, so that if you look on them you look through them; and he that peeps through the casement of the index sees as much as if he were in the house. But the laziness of those cannot be excused who perfunctorily pass over authors of consequence, and only trade in their tables of contents. These, like city-cheaters, having gotten the names of all country gentlemen, make silly people believe they have long lived in those places where they never were, and flourish with skill in those authors they never seriously studied.

The genius of the author is commonly discovered in the dedicatory epistle. Many place the purest grain in the mouth of the sack for chapmen to handle or buy; and from the dedication one may probably guess at the work, saving some rare and peculiar exceptions. Thus, when once a gentleman admired how so pithy, learned, and witty a dedication was matched to a flat, dull, foolish book: "In truth," said another, "they may be well matched together, for I profess they are nothing akin."

Proportion an hour's meditation to an hour's reading of a staple author. This makes a man master of his learning, and dispirits the book into the scholar. The King of Sweden never filed his men above six deep in one company, because he would not have them lie in useless clusters in his army, but so that every particular soldier might be drawn out into service. Books that stand thin on the shelves, yet so as the owner of them can bring forth every one of them into use, are better than far greater libraries.

Learning hath gained most by those books by which the printers have lost. Arias Montanus, in printing the Hebrew Bible, (commonly called the Bible of the King of Spain,) much wasted himself, and was accused in the court of Rome for his good deed, and being cited thither, *pro tantorum laborum præmio vix veniam impetravit.* Likewise, Christopher Plantin, by printing of his curious interlineary Bible in Antwerp, through the unseasonable exactions of the king's officers, sunk and almost ruined his estate. And our worthy English knight, who set forth the golden-mouthed Father* in a silver print, was a loser by it.

* Chrysostom.

Whereas foolish pamphlets prove most beneficial to the printers. When a French printer complained that he was utterly undone by printing a solid serious book of Rabelais concerning physic, Rabelais, to make him recompense, made that his jesting, scurrilous work, which repaired the printer's loss with advantage. Such books the world swarms too much with. When one had set out a witless pamphlet, writing *Finis* at the end thereof, another wittily wrote beneath it,

——— "Nay, there thou liest, my friend,
In writing foolish books there is no end."

And surely such scurrilous, scandalous papers do more than conceivable mischief. First, their lusciousness puts many palates out of taste, that they can never after relish any solid and wholesome writers; secondly, they cast dirt on the faces of many innocent persons, which, dried on by continuance of time, can never after be washed off; thirdly, the pamphlets of this age may pass for records with the next, (because publicly uncontrolled,) and what we laugh at, our children may believe; fourthly, grant the things true they jeer at, yet this music is unlawful in any Christian church, to play upon the sins and miseries of others, the fitter object of the elegies than the satires of all truly religious.

But what do I, speaking against multiplicity

of books in this age, who trespass in this nature myself? What was a learned man's * compliment, may serve for my confession and conclusion:—*Multi mei similes hoc morbo laborant, ut cum scribere nesciant, tamen a scribendo temperare non possint.*

OF TIME-SERVING.

THERE be four kinds of time-serving: first, out of Christian discretion, which is commendable; second, out of human infirmity, which is more pardonable; third, and fourth, out of ignorance, or affectation, both which are damnable: of them in order.

He is a good time-server that complies his manners to the several ages of this life: pleasant in youth, without wantonness; grave in old age, without frowardness. Frost is as proper for winter as flowers for spring. Gravity becomes the ancient; and a green Christmas is neither handsome nor healthful.

He is a good time-server that finds out the fittest opportunity for every action. God hath made "a time for everything under the sun," save only for that which we do at all times, to wit, sin.

* Erasmus.

He is a good time-server that improves the present for God's glory and his own salvation. Of all the extent of time, only the instant is that which we can call ours.

He is a good time-server that is pliant to the times in matters of mere indifferency. To blame are they whose minds may seem to be made of one entire bone without any joints: they cannot bend at all, but stand as stiffly in things of pure indifferency as in matters of absolute necessity.

He is a good time-server that in time of persecution neither betrays God's cause nor his own safety. And this he may do,

1. By lying hid both in his person and practice: though he will do no evil, he will forbear the public doing of some good. He hath as good cheer in his heart, though he keeps not open house, and will not publicly broach his religion, till the palate of the times be better in taste to relish it. "The prudent shall keep silence in that time, for it is an evil time;" though according to St. Peter's command we are to "give a reason of our hope to every one that asketh," namely, that asketh for his instruction, but not for our destruction, especially if wanting lawful authority to examine us. "Ye shall be brought," saith Christ, (no need have they therefore to run,) "before princes for my sake."

2. By flying away: if there be no absolute necessity of his staying, no scandal given by his flight; if he wants strength to stay it out till death; and, lastly, if God openeth a fair way for his departure: otherwise, if God bolts the doors and windows against him, he is not to creep out at the top of the chimney, and to make his escape by unwarrantable courses. If all should fly, truth would want champions for the present; if none should fly, truth might want champions for the future. We come now to time-servers out of infirmity.

Heart of oak hath sometimes warped a little in the scorching heat of persecution. Their want of true courage herein cannot be excused. Yet many censure them for surrendering up their forts after a long siege, who would have yielded up their own at the first summons. Oh, there is more required to make one valiant than to call Cranmer or Jewell coward, as if the fire in Smithfield had been no hotter than what is painted in the Book of Martyrs.

Yet afterwards they have come into their former straightness and stiffness. The troops which at first rather wheeled about than ran away, have come in seasonable at last. Yea, their constant blushing for shame of their former cowardliness hath made their souls ever after look more modest and beautiful. Thus Cranmer, who subscribed to Popery, grew valiant afterwards, and thrust his right hand which subscribed first into fire, so that that hand died (as it were) a malefactor, and all the rest of his body died a martyr.

Some have served the times out of mere ignorance; gaping for company, as others gaped before them, "*Pater Noster*," or, "Our Father." I could both sigh and smile at the witty simplicity of a poor old woman who had lived in the days of Queen Mary and Queen Elizabeth, and said her prayers daily both in Latin and English, and "let God," said she, "take to himself which he likes best."

But worst are those who serve the times out of mere affectation; doing as the times do, not because the times do as they should do, but merely for sinister respects, to ingratiate themselves. We read of an Earl of Oxford fined by King Henry the Seventh fifteen thousand marks for having too many retainers. But how many retainers hath time had in all ages? and servants in all offices? yea, and chaplains too?

It is a very difficult thing to serve the times; they change so frequently, so suddenly, and sometimes so violently from one extreme to another. The times under Diocletian were Pagan; under Constantine, Christian; under Constantius, Arian; under Julian, Apostate; under Jovian, Christian again; and all within the age of man, the term of seventy years.

And would it not have wrenched and sprained his soul with short turning, who in all these should have been of the religion for the time being?

Time-servers are oftentimes left in the lurch; if they do not only give their word for the times in their constant discourses, but also give their bonds for them, and write in their defence. Such, when the times turn afterwards to another extreme, are left in the briers, and come off very hardly from the bill of their hands; if they turn again with the times, none will trust them; for who will make a staff of an osier?

Miserable will be the condition of such time-servers when their master is taken from them; when, as the angel swore, (*Rev.* x. 6,) that "time shall be no longer." Therefore is it best serving of him who is eternity, a master that can ever protect us.

To conclude: he that intends to meet with one in a great fair, and knows not where he is, may sooner find him by standing still in some principal place there, than by traversing it up and down. Take thy stand on some good ground in religion, and keep thy station in a fixed posture, never hunting after the times to follow them, and an hundred to one they will come to thee once in thy lifetime.

OF MODERATION.

MODERATION "is the silken string running through the pearl-chain of all virtues."* It appears both in practice and judgment: we will insist on the latter, and describe it first negatively.

Moderation is not a halting betwixt two opinions, when the through-believing of one of them is necessary to salvation: no pity is to be shown to such voluntary cripples. We read (*Acts* xxvii. 12) of a haven in Crete, which lay towards the southwest and towards the northwest: strange, that it could have part of two opposite points, north and south: sure, it must be very winding. And thus some men's souls are in such intricate postures, they lay towards the Papists and towards the Protestants: such we count not of a moderate judgment, but of an immoderate unsettledness.

Nor is it a lukewarmness in those things wherein God's glory is concerned. Herein it 's a true rule, *Non amat qui non zelat.* And they that are thus lukewarm here shall be too hot hereafter in that oven wherein dough-baked cakes shall be burnt.

But it is a mixture of discretion and charity in one's judgment. Discretion puts a difference

* Bishop Hall.

betwixt things absolutely necessary to salvation to be done and believed, and those which are of a second sort and lower form, wherein more liberty and latitude is allowed. In maintaining whereof, the stiffness of the judgment is abated, and suppled with charity towards his neighbor. The lukewarm man eyes only his own ends and particular profit; the moderate man aims at the good of others, and unity of the church.

Yet such moderate men are commonly crushed betwixt the extreme parties on both sides. But what said Ignatius? "I am Christ's wheat, and must be ground with the teeth of beasts, that I may be made God's pure manchet." Saints are born to suffer, and must take it patiently. Besides, in this world generally they get the least preferment; it faring with them as with the guest that sat in the midst of the table, who could reach to neither mess, above or beneath him: —

> "Esuriunt medii, fines bene sunt saturati;
> Dixerunt stulti, medium tenuere beati."

> "Both ends o' th' table furnished are with meat,
> Whilst they in middle nothing have to eat.
> They were none of the wisest well I wist,
> Who made bliss in the middle to consist."

Yet these temporal inconveniences of moderation are abundantly recompensed with other better benefits: for

1. A well-informed judgment in itself is a preferment. Potamon began a sect of philoso-

phers called ἐκλεκτικοὶ, who wholly adhered to no former sect, but chose out of all of them what they thought best. Surely such divines, who in unimporting controversies extract the probablest opinions from all professions, are best at ease in their minds.

2. As the moderate man's temporal hopes are not great, so his fears are the less. He fears not to have the splinters of his party (when it breaks) fly into his eyes, or to be buried under the ruins of his side, if supprest. He never pinned his religion on any man's sleeve, no, not on "the arm of flesh," and therefore is free from all dangerous engagements.

3. His conscience is clear from raising schisms in the Church. The Turks did use to wonder much at our Englishmen for pinking or cutting their clothes, counting them little better than mad for their pains to make holes in whole cloth, which time of itself would tear too soon. But grant men may do with their own garments as their fancy adviseth them, yet woe be to such who willingly cut and rend the seamless coat of Christ with dissensions.

4. His religion is more constant and durable; being here, *in via*, in his way to heaven, and jogging on a good traveller's pace, he overtakes and outgoes many violent men, whose over-hot, ill-grounded zeal was quickly tired.

5. In matters of moment, indeed, none are more zealous. He thriftily treasured up his spirits for that time, who, if he had formerly rent his lungs for every trifle, he would have wanted breath in points of importance.

6. Once in an age the moderate man is in fashion: each extreme courts him to make them friends; and surely he hath a great advantage to be a peace-maker betwixt opposite parties. Now whilst, as we have said, moderate men are constant to themselves,

Violent men reel from one extremity to another. Who would think that the East and West Indies were so near together, whose names speak them at diametrical opposition? And yet their extremities are either the same continent, or parted with a very narrow sea. As the world is round, so we may observe a circulation in opinions, and violent men turn often round in their tenets.

Pride is the greatest enemy to moderation. This makes men stickle for their opinions, to make them fundamental. Proud men, having deeply studied some additional point in divinity, will strive to make the same necessary to salvation, to enhance the value of their own worth and pains; and it must be fundamental in religion, because it is fundamental to their reputation. Yea, as love doth descend, and men dote most on their grandchildren, so these are indulgent to the deductions of their deductions, and consequential inferences to the seventh generation, making them all of the foundation, though scarce of the building of religion. Ancient Fathers made the creed *symbolum* the shot and total sum of faith. Since which, how many arrearages and after-reckonings have men brought us in? to which if we will not pay our belief, our souls must be arrested without bail upon pain of damnation. Next to pride, popular applause is the greatest foe moderation hath, and sure they who sail with that wind have their own vainglory for their haven.

To close up all, let men, on God's blessing, soundly, yet wisely, whip and lash lukewarmness and time-serving, their thongs will never fly in the face of true moderation, to do it any harm; for, however men may undervalue it, that Father spake most truly,—*Si virtutum finis ille sit maximus, qui plurimorum spectat profectum, moderatio prope omnium pulcherrima est.*

OF GRAVITY.

GRAVITY is the ballast of the soul, which keeps the mind steady. It is either true or counterfeit.

Natural dulness and heaviness of temper is

sometimes mistaken for true gravity in such men in whose constitutions one of the tetrarch elements, fire, may seem to be omitted. These sometimes not only cover their defects, but get praise:

"Sæpe latet vitium proximitate boni."

They do wisely to counterfeit a reservedness, and to keep their chests always locked, not for fear any should steal treasure thence, but lest some should look in and see that there is nothing within them. Wonder not so much that such men are grave, but wonder at them if they be not grave.

Affected gravity passes often for that which is true: I mean with dull eyes, for in itself nothing is more ridiculous; when one shall use the preface of a mile to bring in a furlong of matter, set his face and speech in a frame, and to make men believe it is some precious liquor, their words come out drop by drop. Such men's vizards do sometimes fall from them, not without the laughter of the beholders. One was called "gravity" for his affected solemness, who afterwards being catched in a light prank, was ever after to the day of his death called "gravity-levity."

True gravity expresseth itself in gait, gesture, apparel, and speech. *Vox quædam est animi, corporis motus.* As for speech, gravity enjoins it,

1. Not to be over-much. "In the multitude of words there wanteth not sin." For of necessity many of them must be idle whose best commendation is that they are good for nothing. Besides, *dum otiosa verba cavere negligimus, ad noxia pervenimus.* And great talkers discharge too thick to take always true aim; besides, it is odious in a company. A man full of words, who took himself to be a grand wit, made his brag that he was the leader of the discourse in what company soever he came, and "None," said he, "dare speak in my presence, if I hold my peace." "No wonder," answered one, "for they are all struck dumb at the miracle of your silence."

2. To be wise and discreet. *Colossians* iv. 6, "Let your speech be always with grace, seasoned with salt:" always—not only sometimes, in the company of godly men. Tindal's being in the room hindered a juggler that he could not play his feats: (a saint's presence stops the devil's elbow-room to do his tricks:) and so some wicked men are awed into good discourse whilst pious people are present. But it must be always "seasoned with salt," which is the *primum vivens et ultimum moriens* at a feast, first brought and last taken away, and set in the midst as most necessary thereunto. "With salt," that is with wisdom and discretion, *non salibus, sed sale;* nor yet with smart-

ing jeers, like those whose discourse is fire-salt, speaking constant satires to the disgrace of others.

That may be done privately without breach of gravity, which may not be done publicly; as when a father makes himself his child's rattle, sporting with him till the father hath devoured the wise man in him:

> "Equitans in arundine longa."
>
> Instead of stately steed,
> Riding upon a reed.

Making play unto him, that one would think he killed his own discretion, to bring his child asleep. Such cases are no trespass on gravity; and married men may claim their privilege, to be judged by their peers, and may herein appeal from the censuring verdict of bachelors.

Nature in men is sometimes unjustly taxed for a trespass against gravity. Some have active spirits, yea, their ordinary pace is a race. Others have so scornful a carriage that he who seeth them once may think them to be all pride, whilst he that seeth them often knows them to have none. Others have, perchance, a misbeseeming garb in gesture which they cannot amend; that fork needing strong tines wherewith one must thrust away nature. A fourth sort are of a merry, cheerful disposition; and God forbid all such should be condemned for lightness. O let not any envious eye disinherit men of that which is their portion in this life, comfortably to enjoy the blessings thereof. Yet gravity must prune, though not root out our mirth.

Gracious deportment may sometimes unjustly be accused of lightness. Had one seen David dancing before the ark, Elijah in his praying posture when he put his head betwixt his legs, perchance he might have condemned them of unfitting behavior. Had he seen Peter and John posting to Christ's grave, Rhoda running into the house, he would have thought they had left their gravity behind them. But let none blame them for their speed, until he knows what were their spurs, and what were the motives that urged them to make such haste. These their actions were the true conclusions following from some inward premises in their own souls; and that may be a syllogism in grace which appears a solecism in manners.

In some persons gravity is most necessary, viz: in magistrates and ministers. One Palevizine, an Italian gentleman, and kinsman to Scaliger, had in one night all his hair changed from black to gray. Such an alteration ought there to be in the heads of every one that enters into holy orders, or public office, metamorphosed from all lightness to gravity.

God alone is the giver of true gravity. No

man wants so much of any grace as he hath to spare; and a constant impression of God's omnipresence is an excellent way to fix men's souls. Bishop Andrews ever placed the picture of Mulcaster, his schoolmaster, over the door of his study (whereas in all the rest of his house you should scarce see a picture), as to be his tutor and supervisor. Let us constantly apprehend God's being in presence, and this will fright us into staid behavior.

OF MARRIAGE.

SOME men have too much decried marriage. Give this holy estate her due, and then we shall find,

Though bachelors be the strongest stakes, married men are the best binders in the hedge of the commonwealth. 'T is the policy of the Londoners, when they send a ship into the Levant or Mediterranean Sea, to make every mariner therein a merchant, each seaman adventuring somewhat of his own, which will make him more wary to avoid, and more valiant to undergo dangers. Thus married men, especially if having posterity, are the deeper sharers in that state wherein they live, which engageth their affections to the greater loyalty.

It is the worst clandestine marriage when God is not invited to it. Wherefore beforehand beg his gracious assistance. Marriage shall prove no lottery to thee, when the hand of Providence chooseth for thee, who, if drawing a blank, can turn it into a prize, by sanctifying a bad wife unto thee.

Deceive not thyself by over-expecting happiness in the married estate. Look not therein for contentment greater than God will give, or a creature in this world can receive, namely, to be free from all inconveniences. Marriage is not like the hill Olympus, ὅλος λαμπρός, wholly clear, without clouds. Yea, expect both wind and storms sometimes, which, when blown over, the air is the clearer and wholesomer for it. Make account of certain cares and troubles which will attend thee. Remember the nightingales, which sing only some months in the spring, but commonly are silent when they have hatched their eggs, as if their mirth were turned into care for their young ones. Yet all the molestations of marriage are abundantly recompensed with other comforts which God bestoweth on them who make a wise choice of a wife, and observe the following rules:

Let grace and goodness be the principal loadstone of thy affections. For love which hath ends will have an end, whereas that which is founded in true virtue will always continue. Some hold it unhappy to be married with a diamond ring; perchance, (if there be so much reason in their folly,) because the diamond hinders the roundness of the ring, ending the infiniteness thereof, and seems to presage some termination in their love, which ought ever to endure, and so it will, when it is founded in religion.

Neither choose all, nor not at all for beauty. A cried-up beauty makes more for her own praise than her husband's profit. They tell us of a floating island in Scotland: but sure no wise pilot will cast anchor there, lest the land swim away with his ship. So are they served, and justly enough, who only fasten their love on fading beauty, and both fail together.

Let there be no great disproportion in age. They that marry ancient people merely in expectation to bury them, hang themselves in hope that one will come and cut the halter.

Let wealth in its due distance be regarded. There be two towns in the land of Liege, called Bovins and Dinant, the inhabitants whereof bear almost an incredible hatred one to another, and yet, notwithstanding, their children usually marry together; and the reason is, because there is none other good town or wealthy place near them. Thus parents for a little pelf often marry their children to those whose persons they hate; and thus union betwixt families is not made, but the breach rather widened the more.

This shall serve for a conclusion. A bachelor was saying, "Next to no wife, a good wife is best." "Nay," said a gentlewoman, "next to a good wife, no wife is the best." I wish to all married people the outward happiness which, *anno* 1605, happened to a couple in the city of Delft in Holland, living most lovingly together seventy-five years in wedlock, till the man being one hundred and three, the woman ninety-nine years of age, died within three hours each of other, and were buried in the same grave.

OF FAME.

FAME is the echo of actions, resounding them to the world, save that the echo repeats only the last part, but fame relates all, and often more than all.

Fame sometimes hath created something of nothing. She hath made whole countries more than ever nature did, especially near the poles, and then hath peopled them likewise with inhabitants of her own invention, — pigmies, giants, and amazons. Yea, fame is sometimes like unto a kind of mushroom, which Pliny recounts to be the greatest miracle in nature, because growing and having no root, as fame no ground for her reports.

Fame often makes a great deal of a little. Absalom killed one of David's sons, and fame killed all the rest; and, generally, she magnifies and multiplies matters. Loud was that lie which that bell told, hanging in a clock-house at Westminster, and usually rung at the coronation and funerals of princes, having this inscription about it, —

> "King Edward made me
> Thirty thousand and three;
> Take me down and weigh me,
> And more shall you find me."

But when this bell was taken down at the doomsday of abbeys, this and two more were found not to weigh twenty thousand. Many relations of fame are found to shrink accordingly.

Some fames are most difficult to trace home to their form; and those who have sought to track them have gone rather in a circle than forward, and oftentimes, through the doubling of reports, have returned back again where they began.

Politicians sometimes raise fames on purpose; as that such things are done already which they mean to do afterwards. By the light of those false fires they see into men's hearts, and these false rumors are true scouts to discover men's dispositions. Besides, the deed, though strange in itself, is done afterwards with the less noise, men having vented their wonder beforehand, and the strangeness of the action is abated, because formerly made stale in report. But if the rumor startles men extremely, and draws with it dangerous consequences, then they can presently confute it, let their intentions fall, and prosecute it no further.

The Papal side of all fame-merchants drive the most gainful trade, as that worthy knight, Sir Edward Sandys, hath given us an exact survey thereof. But long before them, strange was that plot of Stratocles, who gave it out that he had gotten a victory, and the constant report thereof continued three days, and then was confuted; and Stratocles being charged with abusing his people with a lie, "Why," said he, "are ye angry with me for making you pass three days in mirth and jollity more than otherwise you should?"

Incredible is the swiftness of Fame in carrying reports. First she creeps through a village, then she goes through a town, then she runs through a city, then she flies through a country, — still the farther the faster. Yea, Christ, who made the dumb speak, made not tell-tale Fame silent, though charging those he cured to hold their peace; "but so much the more went there a fame abroad of him." Yea, some things have been reported soon as ever they were done, at impossible distance. The overthrow of Perseus was brought out of Macedon to Rome in four days. And in Domitian's time, a report was brought two thousand five hundred miles in one day. In which accidents,

1. Fame takes post on some other advantage. Thus the overthrow of the Sabines was known at Rome, *prius pene quam nunciari possit*, by the means of the arms of the Sabines drowned in the river of Tiber, and carried down by the tide to Rome. And thus, *anno* 1568, the overthrow which the Spaniards gave the Dutch at the river of Ems, was known at Grunning before any horseman could reach thither, by the multitude of the Dutch caps which the river brought down into the city. But these conveyances are but slugs to make such miraculous speed: wherefore sometimes reports are carried,

2. By the ministration of spirits. The devils are well at leisure to play such pranks, and may do it in a frolic. And yet they would scarce be the carriers except they were well paid for the portage, getting some profit thereby, (doing of mischief is all the profit they are capable of,) and do harm to some by the suddenness of those reports. Or else,

3. The fame is antedated and raised before the fact, being related at guess before it was acted. Thus some have been causelessly commended for early rising in the morning, who indeed came to their journey's end overnight. If such fore-made reports prove true, they are admired and registered; if false, neglected and forgotten: as those only which escaped shipwreck hung up *votivas tabulas*, tablets with their names, in those haven-towns where they came ashore; but as for those who are drowned, their memorials are drowned with them.

General reports are seldom false. *Vox populi vox Dei.* A body of that greatness hath an eye of like clearness, and it is impossible that a wanderer with a counterfeit pass should pass undiscovered.

A fond fame is best confuted by neglecting it. By fond, understand such a report as is rather ridiculous than dangerous if believed. It is not worth the making a schism betwixt news-mongers, to set up an anti-fame against it. Yea, seriously and studiously to endeavor to confute it, will grace the rumor too much, and give suspicion that indeed there is some reality in it. What madness were it to plant a piece of ordnance to beat down an aspen leaf, which, having always the palsy, will at last fall down of itself. And Fame hath much of the scold in her; the best way to silence her is to be silent, and then at last she will be out of breath with blowing her own trumpet.

Fame sometimes reports things less than they are. Pardon her for offending herein, she is guilty so seldom. For one kingdom of Scotland, which, they say, geographers describe an hundred miles too short, most northern countries are made too large. Fame generally overdoes, underdoes but in some particulars. The Italian proverb hath it, "There is less honesty, wisdom, and money in men than is counted on;" yet sometimes a close churl, who locks his coffers so fast Fame could never peep into them, dieth richer than he was reported when alive. None could come near to feel his estate; it might therefore cut fatter in his purse than was expected. But Fame falls most short in those transcendents which are above her predicaments: as in Solomon's wisdom, "And behold, one half was not told me; thy wisdom and prosperity exceedeth the fame that I heard:" but chiefly in fore-reporting the happiness in heaven, which "eye hath not seen, nor ear heard, neither hath it entered into the heart of man to conceive."

OF MINISTERS' MAINTENANCE.

MAINTENANCE of ministers ought to be plentiful, certain, and in some sort proportionable to their deserts. It should be plentiful, because

Their education was very chargeable to fit them for their profession, both at school and in the university: their books very dear, and those which they bought in folio, shrink quickly into quartos, in respect of the price their executors can get for them. Say not that scholars draw needless expenses on themselves by their own lavishness, and that they should rather lead a fashion of thrift than follow one of riot; for let any equal man tax the bill of their necessary charges, and it amounts to a great sum, yea, though they be never so good husbands. Besides, the prices of all commodities daily rise higher; all persons and professions are raised in their manner of living. Scholars therefore, even against their wills, must otherwhiles be involved in the general expensiveness of the times; it being impossible that one spoke should stand still when all the wheel turns about.

Objec. But many needlessly charge themselves in living too long in the university, sucking so long of their mother, they are never a whit the wiser for it; whilst others, not staying there so long, nor going through the porch of human arts, but entering into divinity at the postern, have made good preachers, providing their people wholesome meat, though not so finely drest.

Answ. Much good may it do their very hearts that feed on it. But how necessary a competent knowledge of those sciences is for a perfect divine, is known to every wise man. Let not men's suffering be counted their fault, not those accused to stand idle in the market, whom no man hath hired. Many would leave the university sooner, if called into the country on tolerable conditions.

Because ministers are to subsist in a free, liberal, and comfortable way. Balaam, the false prophet, rode with his two men; God's Levite had one man: Oh let not the ministers of the Gospel be slaves to others, and servants to themselves! They are not to pry into gain through every small chink. It becomes them rather to be acquainted with the natures of things than with the prices, and to know them rather as they are in the world than as they are in the market. Otherwise, if his means be small, and living poor, necessity will bolt him out of his own study, and send him to the barn, when he should be at his book, or make him study his Easter-book more than all other writers. Hereupon some wanting what they should have at home, have done what they should not abroad.

Because hospitality is expected at their hands. The poor come to their houses as if they had interest in them, and the ministers can neither receive them nor refuse them. Not to relieve them were not Christianity, and to relieve them were worse than infidelity, because therein they wrong their providing for their own family. Thus sometimes are they forced to be Nabals against their will; yet it grieveth them to send away the people empty. But what shall they do, seeing they cannot multiply their loaves and their fishes? Besides, clergymen are deeply rated to all payments. Oh that their profession were but as highly prized as their estate is valued!

Because they are to provide for their posterity, that after the death of their parents they may live, though not in a high, yet in an honest fashion, neither leaving them to the wide world, nor to a narrow cottage.

Because the Levites in the Old Testament had plentiful provision. Oh 't is good to be God's pensioner, for he giveth his large allowance. They had cities and suburbs, (houses and glebe-land) tithes, freewill-offerings, and their parts in first-fruits, and sacrifices. Do the ministers of the Gospel deserve worse wages for bringing better tidings? Besides, the Levites' places were hereditary, and the son sure of his father's house and land without a faculty *ad succedendum patri.*

Because the Papists in time of Popery gave their priests plentiful means. Whose benefactors, so bountiful to them, may serve to condemn the covetousness of our age towards God's ministers, in such who have more knowledge and should have more religion.

Objec. But the great means of the clergy in time of Popery was rather wrested than given. The priests melted men's hearts into charity with the scarefire of purgatory; and for justice now to give back what holy fraud had gotten away, is not sacrilege but restitution. And when those grand and vast donations were given to the Church, there was (as some say) a voice of angels heard from heaven, saying, *Hodie venenum in ecclesiam Christi cecidit.*

Answ. If poison then fell into the Church, since hath there a strong antidote been given to expel it, especially in impropriations. Distinguish we betwixt such donations given to uses in themselves merely unlawful and superstitious, as praying for the dead, and the like; and those which *in genere* were given to God's service, though *in specie* some superstitious end were annexed thereto. And grant the former of these to be void in their very granting, yet the latter ought to be rectified and reduced to the true use, and in no case to be alienated from God. Plato saith that in his time it was a proverb amongst children, Τῶν ὀρθῶς δοθέντων οὐκ ἔστιν ἀφαίρεσις: Things that are truly given, must not be taken away again. Sure, as our Saviour set a child in the midst of his disciples to teach them humility, so nowadays a child need be set in the midst of some men to teach them justice. Excellently Luther, "Nisi superesset spolium Ægypti, quod rapuimus Papæ, omnibus ministris verbi fame pereundum esset; quod si sustentandi essent de contributione populi, misere profecto ac duriter viverent. Alimur ergo de spoliis Ægypti collectis sub Papatu, et hoc ipsum tamen quod reliquum est diripitur a magistratu: spoliantur parochiæ et scholæ, non aliter ac si fame necare nos velint."

Objec. But in the pure primitive times the means were least, and ministers the best; and nowadays, does not wealth make them lazy, and poverty keep them painful? Like hawks, they fly best when sharp. The best way to keep the stream of the clergy sweet and clear, is to fence out the tide of wealth from coming unto them.

Answ. Is this our thankfulness to the God of heaven, for turning persecution into peace, in pinching his poor ministers? When the commonwealth now makes a feast, shall neither Zadok the Priest, nor Nathan the Prophet, be invited to it? that so the footsteps of primitive persecution may still remain in these peaceable times, amongst the Papists, in their needless burning of candles; and amongst the Protestants, in the poor means of their ministers. And what if some turn the spurs unto virtue into the stirrups of pride, grow idle and insolent? Let them soundly suffer for it themselves on God's blessing; but let not the bees be starved that the drones may be punished.

Ministers' maintenance ought to be certain; lest some of them meet with Labans for their patrons and parishioners; changing their wages ten times; and at last, if the fear of God doth not fright them, send them away empty.

It is unequal that there should be an equality betwixt all ministers' maintenance; except that first there were made an equality betwixt all their parts, pains, and piety. Parity in means will quickly bring a level and flat in learning; and few will strive to be such spiritual musicians, to whom David directeth many psalms, "to him that excelleth," but will even content themselves with a canonical sufficiency, and desiring no more than what the law requires: more learning would be of more pains, and the same profit, seeing the *mediocriter* goeth abreast with *optime.*

Objec. But neither the best, nor the most painful and learned, get the best preferment.

Sometimes men of the least, get livings of the best worth; yea, such as are not worthy to be the curates to their curates, and *crassa ingenia* go away with *opima sacerdotia.*

Answ. Thus it ever was, and will be. But is this dust only to be found in churches, and not in civil courts? Is merit everywhere else made the exact square of preferment? Or did ever any urge that all offices should be made champaign for their profits, none higher than other? Such corruptions will ever be in the Church, except there were a law (ridiculous to be made, and impossible to be kept) that men should be no men, but that all patrons or people, in their election or presentations of ministers, should wholly divest themselves of by-respects of kindred, friendship, profit, affection, and merely choose for desert; and then should we have all things so well ordered, such pastors and such people, the Church in a manner would be triumphant, whilst militant. Till then, though the best livings light not always on the ablest men, yet as long as there be such preferments in the Church, there are still encouragements for men to endeavor to excel, all hoping, and some happening on advancement.

Objec. But ministers ought to serve God merely for love of himself; and pity but his eyes were out that squints at his own ends in doing God's work.

Answ. Then should God's best saints be blind; for Moses himself had an eye to the recompense of reward. Yea, ministers may look not only on their eternal but on their temporal reward, as motives to quicken their endeavors. And though it be true that grave and pious men do study for learning's sake, and embrace virtue for itself, yet it is as true that youth (which is the season when learning is gotten) is not without ambition, nor will ever take pains to excel in anything, when there is not some hope of excelling others in reward and dignity. And what reason is it, that, whilst law and physic bring great portions to such as marry them, divinity, their eldest sister, should only be put off with her own beauty? In after-ages men will rather bind their sons to one gainful than to seven liberal sciences: only the lowest of the people would be made ministers, which cannot otherwise subsist; and it will be bad when God's Church is made a sanctuary only for men of desperate estates to take refuge in it.

However, let every minister take up this resolution, "to preach the Word, to be instant in season, out of season, reprove, rebuke, exhort with all long-suffering and doctrine." If thou hast competent means comfortably to subsist on, be the more thankful to God the fountain, to man the channel; painful in thy place, pitiful to the poor, cheerful in spending some, careful in keeping the rest. If not, yet tire not for want of a spur: do something for love, and not all for money; for love of God, of goodness, of the godly, of a good conscience. Know 't is better to want means than to detain them; the one only suffers, the other deeply sins; and it is as dangerous a persecution to religion to draw the fuel from it as to cast water on it. Comfort thyself that another world will pay this world's debts, "and great is thy reward with God in heaven;" a reward, in respect of his promise; a gift, in respect of thy worthlessness: and yet the less thou lookest at it, the surer thou shalt find it, if laboring with thyself to serve God for himself, in respect of whom even heaven itself is but a sinister end.

THE PROFANE STATE

THE PROFANE STATE.

THE WITCH.

BEFORE we come to describe her, we must premise and prove certain propositions, whose truth may otherwise be doubted of.

1. Formerly there were witches. Otherwise God's law had fought against a shadow, "Thou shalt not suffer a witch to live." Yea, we read how King Saul, who had formerly scoured witches out of all Israel, afterwards drank a draught of that puddle himself.

2. There are witches for the present, though those night-birds fly not so frequently in flocks, since the light of the Gospel. Some ancient arts and mysteries are said to be lost; but sure the devil will not wholly let down any of his gainful trades. There be many witches at this day in Lapland, who sell winds to mariners for money, (and must they not needs go whom the devil drives?) though we are not

bound to believe the old story of Ericus, King of Swedeland, who had a cap, and as he turned it, the wind he wished for would blow on that side.

3. It is very hard to prove a witch. Infernal contracts are made without witnesses. She that in presence of others will compact with the devil, deserves to be hanged for her folly as well as impiety.

4. Many are unjustly accused for witches: sometimes out of ignorance of natural, and misapplying of supernatural causes; sometimes out of their neighbors' mere malice, and the suspicion is increased if the party accused be notoriously ill-favored; whereas deformity alone is no more argument to make her a witch than handsomeness had been evidence to prove her a harlot; sometimes out of their own causeless confession: being brought before a magistrate, they acknowledge themselves to be witches, being themselves rather bewitched with fear or deluded with fancy. But the self-accusing of some is as little to be credited as the self-praising of others, if alone without other evidence.

5. Witches are commonly of the feminine sex. Ever since Satan tempted our grandmother Eve, he knows that that sex is most lickerish to taste, and most careless to swallow his baits. *Nescio quid habet muliebre nomen*

semper cum sacris: If they light well, they are inferior to few men in piety; if ill, superior to all in superstition.

6. They are commonly distinguished into white and black witches. White, I dare not say good, witches (for woe be to him that calleth evil good) heal those that are hurt, and help them to lost goods. But better it is to lap one's pottage like a dog than to eat it mannerly with a spoon of the devil's giving. Black witches hurt, and do mischief. But in deeds of darkness there is no difference of colors: the white and the black are both guilty alike in compounding with the devil. And now we come to see by what degrees people arrive at this height of profaneness.

At the first, she is only ignorant and very malicious. She hath usually a bad face and a worse tongue, given to railing and cursing, as if constantly bred on Mount Ebal; yet speaking perchance worse than she means, though meaning worse than she should. And as the harmless wapping of a cursed cur may stir up a fierce mastiff to the worrying of sheep, so, on her cursing, the devil may take occasion by God's permission to do mischief, without her knowledge, and perchance against her will.

Some have been made witches by endeavoring to defend themselves against witchcraft; for fearing some suspected witch should hurt them, they fence themselves with the devil's shield against the devil's sword, put on his whole armor, beginning to use spells and charms to safeguard themselves. The art is quickly learnt, to which nothing but credulity and practice is required; and they often fall from defending themselves to offending of others, especially the devil not being dainty of his company where he finds welcome; and being invited once, he haunts ever after.

She begins at first with doing tricks rather strange than hurtful; yea, some of them are pretty and pleasing. But it is dangerous to gather flowers that grow on the banks of the pit of hell, for fear of falling in; yea, they which play with the devil's rattles will be brought by degrees to wield his sword, and from making of sport they come to doing of mischief.

At last she indents downright with the devil. He is to find her some toys for a time, and to have her soul in exchange. At the first (to give the devil his due) he observes the agreement, to keep up his credit, else none would trade with him; though at last he either deceives her with an equivocation, or at some other small hole this serpent winds out himself, and breaks the covenants. And where shall she, poor wretch, sue the forfeited bond? In heaven she neither can nor dare appear; on earth she is hanged if the contract be proved; in hell her adversary is judge, and it is woful to appeal from the devil to the devil. But for a while let us behold her in her supposed felicity.

She taketh her free progress from one place to another. Sometimes the devil doth locally transport her; but he will not be her constant hackney to carry such luggage about; but oftentimes, to save portage, deludes her brains in her sleep, so that they brag of long journeys whose heads never travelled from their bolsters. These, with Drake, sail about the world, but it is on an ocean of their own fancies, and in a ship of the same. They boast of brave banquets they have been at, but they would be very lean should they eat no other meat. Others will persuade, if any list to believe, that by a witch-bridle they can make a fair of horses of an acre of besom-weed. Oh silly souls! Oh subtle Satan that deceived them!

With strange figures and words she summons the devils to attend her; using a language which God never made at the confusion of tongues, and an interpreter must be fetched from hell to expound it. With these, or Scripture abused, the devil is ready at her service. Who would suppose that a roaring lion could so finely act the spaniel? One would think he were too old to suck, and yet he will do that also for advantage.

Sometimes she enjoins him to do more for her than he is able; as to wound those whom God's providence doth arm, or to break through the tents of blessed angels, to hurt one of God's saints. Here Satan is put to his shifts, and his wit must help him where his power fails; he either excuseth it, or seemingly performs it, lengthening his own arm by the dimness of her eye, and presenting the seeming bark of that tree which he cannot bring.

She lives commonly but very poor. Methinks she should bewitch to herself a golden mine, at least good meat and whole clothes. But 't is as rare to see one of her profession, as a hangman, in a whole suit. Is the possession of the devil's favor here no better? Lord, what is the reversion of it hereafter!

When arraigned for her life, the devil leaves her to the law to shift for herself. He hath worn out all his shoes in her former service, and will not now go barefoot to help her; and the circle of the halter is found to be too strong for all her spirits. Yea, Zoroastes himself, the first inventor of magic, though he laughed at his birth, led a miserable life, and died a woful death in banishment.

THE ATHEIST.

THE word *atheist* is of a very large extent. Every polytheist is in effect an atheist; for he that multiplies a deity, annihilates it; and he that divides it, destroys it.

But amongst the heathen we may observe that whosoever sought to withdraw people from their idolatry, was presently indicted and arraigned of atheism. If any philosopher saw God through their gods, this dust was cast in his eyes, for being more quick-sighted than others, that presently he was condemned for an atheist; and thus Socrates, the Pagan martyr, was put to death ὡς ἄθεος. At this day three sorts of atheists are extant in the world:

1. In life and conversation. *Psal.* x. 4: "God is not in all his thoughts;" not that he thinks there is no God, but thinks not there is a God, never minding or heeding him in the whole course of his life and actions.

2. In will and desire. Such could wish there were no God, or devil; as thieves would have no judge nor jailer; *quod metuunt, periisse expetunt.*

3. In judgment and opinion. Of the former two sorts of atheists, there are more in the world than are generally thought; of this

latter, more are thought to be than there are, a contemplative atheist being very rare, such as were Diagoras, Protagoras, Lucian, and Theodorus, who, though carrying God in his name, was an atheist in his opinion. Come we to see by what degrees a man may climb up to this height of profaneness. And we will suppose him to be one living in wealth and prosperity, which more disposeth men to atheism than adversity; for affliction mindeth men of a deity, as those which are pinched will cry, O Lord! but much outward happiness abused, occasioneth men, as wise Agur observeth, "to deny God, and say, Who is the Lord?"

First, he quarrels at the diversities of religions in the world, complaining how great clerks dissent in their judgments, which makes him sceptical in all opinions; whereas such differences should not make men careless to have any, but careful to have the best religion.

He loveth to maintain paradoxes and to shut his eyes against the beams of a known truth; not only for discourse, which might be permitted, (for, as no cloth can be woven except the woof and the warp be cast cross one to another, so discourse will not be maintained without some opposition for the time,) but our inclining atheist goes further, engaging his affections in disputes, even in such matters where the supposing them wounds piety, but the positive maintaining them stabs it to the heart.

He scoffs and makes sport at sacred things. This, by degrees, abates the reverence of religion, and ulcers men's hearts with profaneness. The Popish proverb, well understood, hath a truth in it, "Never dog barked against the crucifix, but he ran mad."

Hence he proceeds to take exception at God's Word. He keeps a register of many difficult places of Scripture, not that he desires satisfaction therein, but delights to puzzle divines therewith, and counts it a great conquest when he hath posed them. Unnecessary questions out of the Bible are his most necessary study; and he is more curious to know where Lazarus his soul was the four days he lay in the grave, than careful to provide for his own soul when he shall be dead. Thus is it just with God, that they who will not feed on the plain meat of his Word, should be choked with the bones thereof. But his principal delight is to sound the alarum, and to set several places of Scripture to fight one against another, betwixt which there is a seeming, and he would make a real, contradiction.

Afterwards he grows so impudent as to deny the Scripture itself. As Samson being fastened by a web to a pin, carried away both web and pin, so, if any urge our atheist with arguments from Scripture, and tie him to the authority of God's Word, he denies both reason and God's Word, to which the reason is fastened.

Hence he proceeds to deny God himself. First, in his administration; then in his essence. What else could be expected but that he should bite at last who had snarled so long? First, he denies God's ordering of sublunary matters. "Tush, doth the Lord see, or is there knowledge in the Most High?" making him a maimed deity, without an eye of providence, or an arm of power, and at most restraining him only to matters above the clouds. But he that dares to confine the King of heaven, will soon after endeavor to depose him, and fall at last flatly to deny him.

He furnisheth himself with an armory of arguments to fight against his own conscience: some taken from

1. The impunity and outward happiness of wicked men: as the heathen poet, whose verses for me shall pass un-Englished.

> "Esse Deos credamne? fidem jurata fefellit,
> Et facies illi, quæ fuit ante, manet."

And no wonder if an atheist breaks his neck thereat, whereat the foot of David himself (*Psal.* lxxiii. 2, 3) did almost slip when he saw the prosperity of the wicked; whom God only reprieves for punishment hereafter.

2. From the afflictions of the godly, whilst

indeed God only tries their faith and patience. As Absalom complained of his father David's government, that none were deputed to redress people's grievances, so he objects that none righteth the wrongs of God's people, and thinks (proud dust!) the world would be better steered if he were the pilot thereof.

3. From the delaying of the day of judgment, with those mockers, (2 *Peter* iii. 3,) whose objections the apostle fully answereth. And in regard of his own particular, the atheist hath as little cause to rejoice at the deferring of the day of judgment as the thief hath reason to be glad that the assizes be put off, who is to be tried, and may be executed before, at the quarter-sessions: so death may take our atheist off before the day of judgment come.

With these and other arguments he struggles with his own conscience, and long in vain seeks to conquer it, even fearing that Deity he flouts at, and dreading that God whom he denies. And as that famous Athenian soldier, Cynægirus, catching hold of one of the enemy's ships, held it first with his right hand, and when that was cut off, with his left, and when both were cut off, yet still kept it with his teeth, so the conscience of our atheist, though he bruise it and beat it and maim it never so much, still keeps him by the teeth, still feeding and gnawing upon him, torturing and tormenting him with thoughts of a deity which the other desires to suppress.

At last he himself is utterly overthrown by conquering his own conscience. God, in justice, takes from him the light which he thrust from himself, and delivers him up to a seared conscience and a reprobate mind, whereby hell takes possession of him. The apostle saith, (*Acts* xvii. 27,) that a man may feel God in his works; but now our atheist hath a dead palsy, is past all sense, and cannot perceive God who is everywhere presented unto him. It is most strange, yet most true, which is reported, that the arms of the Duke of Rohan, in France, which are fusils or lozenges, are to be seen in the wood or stones throughout all his country; so that break a stone in the middle, or lop a bough of a tree, and one shall behold the grain thereof, by some secret cause in nature, diamonded or streaked in the fashion of a lozenge. Yea, the very same in effect is observed in England; for the resemblances of stars, the arms of the worshipful family of the Shugburies in Warwickshire, are found in the stones within their own manor of Shugbury. But what shall we say? The arms of the God of heaven, namely power, wisdom, and goodness, are to be seen in every creature in the world, even from worms to men; and yet our atheist will not acknowledge them, but ascribes them either to chance, (but could a blind painter limn such curious pictures?) or else to nature, which is a mere sleight of the devil to conceal God from men, by calling him after another name; for what is *natura naturans* but God himself?

His death commonly is most miserable: either burnt, as Diagoras; or eaten up with lice, as Pherecydes; or devoured by dogs, as Lucian; or thunder-shot and turned to ashes, as Olympius. However, descending impenitent into hell, there he is atheist no longer, but hath as much religion as the devil, "to confess God and tremble":

> "Nullus in inferno est atheos, ante fuit."

> "On earth were atheists many,
> In hell there is not any."

All speak truth when they are on the rack; but it is a woful thing to be hell's convert. And there we leave the atheist, having dwelt the longer on his character because that speech of worthy Mr. Greenham deserves to be heeded, "that atheism in England is more to be feared than Popery."

THE HYPOCRITE.

BY hypocrite we understand such a one as doth (*Isaiah* xxxii. 6) "practise hypocrisy," make a trade or work of dissembling; for, otherwise, *hypocriseorum macula carere, aut paucorum est, aut nullorum:* The best of God's children have a smack of hypocrisy.

A hypocrite is himself both the archer and the mark, in all actions shooting at his own praise or profit. And therefore he doth all things that they may be seen; — what with others is held a principal point in law is his main maxim in divinity, — to have good witness. Even fasting itself is meat and drink to him whilst others behold it.

In the outside of religion he outshines a sincere Christian. Gilt cups glitter more than those of massy gold, which are seldom burnished. Yea, well may the hypocrite afford gaudy facing who cares not for any lining; brave it in the shop that hath nothing in the warehouse. Nor is it a wonder if in outward service he outstrips God's servants, who outdoeth God's command by will-worship, giving God more than he requires, though not what most he requires, I mean his heart.

His vizard is commonly plucked off in this world. Sincerity is an entire thing in itself;

hypocrisy consists of several pieces cunningly closed together; and sometimes the hypocrite is smote (as Ahab with an arrow, 1 *Kings* xxii. 34) betwixt the joints of his armor, and so is mortally wounded in his reputation. Now by these shrewd signs a dissembler is often discovered: first, heavy censuring of others for light faults; secondly, boasting of his own goodness; thirdly, the unequal beating of his pulse in matters of piety, — hard, strong, and quick in public actions, — weak, soft, and dull in private matters; fourthly, shrinking in persecution, — for painted faces cannot abide to come nigh the fire.

Yet sometimes he goes to the grave neither detected nor suspected: if masters in their art, and living in peaceable times, wherein piety and prosperity do not fall out, but agree well together. Maud, mother to King Henry the Second, being besieged in Winchester castle, counterfeited herself to be dead, and so was carried out in a coffin, whereby she escaped. Another time, being besieged at Oxford in a cold winter, with wearing white apparel she got away in the snow undiscovered. Thus some hypocrites, by dissembling mortification, that they are dead to the world, and by professing a snow-like purity in their conversations, escape all their lifetime undiscerned by mortal eyes.

By long dissembling piety, he deceives himself at last; yea, he may grow so infatuated as to conceive himself no dissembler, but a sincere saint. A scholar was so possessed with his lively personating of King Richard the Third in a college-comedy, that ever after he was transported with a royal humor in his large expenses, which brought him to beggary, though he had great preferment. Thus the hypocrite, by long acting the part of piety, at last believes himself really to be such a one whom at first he did but counterfeit.

God here knows, and hereafter will make hypocrites known to the whole world. Ottocar, King of Bohemia, refused to do homage to Rodolphus the First, Emperor, till at last, chastised with war, he was content to do him homage privately in a tent; which tent was so contrived by the Emperor's servants, that, by drawing one cord, it was all taken away, and so Ottocar presented on his knees doing his homage to the view of three armies in presence. Thus God at last shall uncase the closest dissembler to the sight of men, angels, and devils, having removed all veils and pretences of piety; no goat in a sheepskin shall steal on his right hand at the last day of judgment.

THE HERETIC.

IT is very difficult accurately to define him. Amongst the heathen, atheist was, and amongst Christians, heretic is, the disgraceful word of course always cast upon those who dissent from the predominant current of the time. Thus those who, in matters of opinion, varied from the Pope's copy the least hair-stroke, are condemned for heretics. Yea, Virgilius, Bishop of Saltzburg, was branded with that censure, for maintaining that there were antipodes opposite to the then known world. It may be, as Alexander, hearing the philosophers dispute of more worlds, wept that he had conquered no part of them; so it grieved the Pope that these antipodes were not subject to his jurisdiction, which much incensed his Holiness against that strange opinion. We will branch the description of a heretic into these three parts.

1. He is one that formerly hath been of the true Church: "They went out from us, but they were not of us." These afterwards prove more offensive to the Church than very Pagans; as the English-Irish, descended anciently of English parentage, (be it spoken with the more shame to them, and sorrow to us,) turning wild, become worse enemies to our nation than the native Irish themselves.

2. Maintaining a fundamental error. Every scratch in the hand is not a stab to the heart; nor doth every false opinion make a heretic.

3. With obstinacy; which is the dead flesh, making the green wound of an error fester into the old sore of a heresy.

It matters not much what manner of person he hath: if beautiful, perchance the more attractive of feminine followers; if deformed, so that his body is as odd as his opinions, he is the more properly entitled to the reputation of crooked saint.

His natural parts are quick and able. Yet he that shall ride on a winged horse to tell him thereof, shall but come too late to bring him stale news of what he knew too well before.

Learning is necessary in himself, if he trades in a critical error; but if he only broaches dregs, and deals in some dull, sottish opinion, a trowel will serve as well as a pencil to daub on such thick, coarse colors. Yea, in some heresies, deep studying is so useless, that the first thing they learn is to inveigh against all learning.

However, some smattering in the original tongues will do well. On occasion he will let fly whole volleys of Greek and Hebrew words, whereby he not only amazeth his ignorant auditors, but also in conferences daunteth many of his opposers, who (though in all other learning far his superiors) may perchance be conscious of want of skill in those languages, whilst the heretic hereby gains credit to his cause and person.

His behavior is seemingly very pious and devout. How foul soever the postern and backdoor be, the gate opening to the street is swept and garnished, and his outside adorned with pretended austerity.

He is extremely proud and discontented with the times, quarrelling that many beneath him in piety are above him in place. This pride hath caused many men, which otherwise might have been shining lights, prove smoking firebrands in the Church.

Having first hammered the heresy in himself, he then falls to seducing of others: so hard it is for one to have the itch and not to scratch. Yea, Babylon herself will allege that for Zion's sake she will not hold her peace. The necessity of propagating the truth is error's plea to divulge her falsehoods. Men, as naturally they desire to know, so they desire what they know should be known.

If challenged to a private dispute, his impudence bears him out. He counts it the only error to confess he hath erred. His face is of brass, which may be said either ever or never to blush. In disputing, his *modus* is *sine modo;* and, as if all figures (even in logic) were magical, he neglects all forms of reasoning, counting that the only syllogism which is his conclusion.

THE LIAR

IS one that makes a trade to tell falsehoods with intent to deceive. He is either open or secret. A secret liar or equivocator is such a one as by mental reservations and other tricks deceives him to whom he speaks, being lawfully called to deliver all the truth; and sure speech being but a copy of the heart, it cannot be avouched for a true copy that hath less in it than the original. Hence it often comes to pass,

> "When Jesuits unto us answer, Nay,
> They do not English speak, 't is Greek they say."

Such an equivocator we leave, more needing a book than character to describe him. The open liar is first, either mischievous, condemned by all; secondly, officious, unlawful also, because doing ill for good to come of it; thirdly, jesting, when in sport and merriment. And though some count a jesting lie to be like the dirt of oysters, which (they say) never stains, yet is it a sin in earnest. What policy is it for one to wound himself to tickle others, and to stab his own soul to make the standers-by sport? We come to describe the liar.

At first he tells a lie with some shame and reluctancy. For then if he cuts off but a lap of truth's garment, his heart smites him; but in process of time he conquers his conscience, and from quenching it there ariseth a smoke which soots and fouls his soul, so that afterwards he lies without any regret.

Having made one lie, he is fain to make more to maintain it. For an untruth, wanting a firm foundation, needs many buttresses. The honor and happiness of the Israelites is the misery and mischief of lies, "Not one amongst them shall be barren," but miraculously procreative to beget others.

He hath a good memory which he badly abuseth. Memory in a liar is no more than needs. For, first, lies are hard to be remembered, because many, whereas truth is but one; secondly, because a lie, cursorily told, takes little footing and settled fastness in the teller's memory, but prints itself deeper in the hearers', who take the greater notice because of the improbability and deformity thereof; and one will remember the sight of a monster longer than the sight of a handsome body. Hence comes it to pass, that, when the liar hath forgotten himself, his auditors put him in mind of the lie, and take him therein.

Sometimes, though his memory cannot help him from being arrested for lying, his wit rescues him; which needs a long reach to bring all ends presently and probably together, gluing the splinters of his tales so cunningly that the cracks cannot be perceived. Thus a relic-monger bragged he could show a feather of the dove at Christ's baptism; but being to show it to the people, a wag had stolen away the feather and put a coal in the room of it. "Well," quoth he to the spectators, "I cannot be so good as my word for the present, but here is one of the coals that broiled St. Lawrence, and that 's worth the seeing."

Being challenged for telling a lie, no man is more furiously angry. Then he draws his sword and threatens, because he thinks that an offer of revenge, to show himself moved at the accusation, doth in some sort discharge him of the imputation; as if the condemning of the sin in appearance acquitted him in effect; or else because he that is called a liar to his face is also called a coward in the same breath, if he swallows it; and the party charged doth conceive that if he vindicates his valor, his truth will be given him into the bargain.

At last, he believes his own lies to be true. He hath told them over and over so often, that prescription makes a right; and he verily believes that at the first he gathered the story out of some authentical author, which only grew in his own brain.

No man else believes him when he speaks the truth. How much gold soever he hath in his chest, his word is but brass and passeth for nothing; yea, he is dumb in effect, for it is all one whether one cannot speak or cannot be believed.

To conclude: some of the West Indians, to expiate their sin of lying, used to let themselves blood in their tongues, and to offer the blood to their idols: a good cure for the squinancy, but no satisfaction for lying. God's Word hath taught us better: "What profit is there in my blood?" The true repentance of the party washed in the blood of Christ can only obtain pardon for this sin.

THE COMMON BARRATOR.

A BARRATOR is a horse-leech, that only sucks the corrupted blood of the law. He trades only in tricks and quirks; his highway is in by-paths, and he loveth a cavil better than an argument, an evasion than an answer. There be two kinds of them: either such as fight themselves, or are trumpeters in a battle to set on others. The former is a professed dueller in the law that will challenge any, and in all suit-combats be either principal or second.

References and compositions he hates as bad as a hangman hates a pardon. Had he been a scholar, he would have maintained all paradoxes; if a chirurgeon, he would never have cured a wound, but always kept it raw; if a soldier, he would have been excellent at a siege, nothing but *ejectio firma* would out him.

He is half starved in the lent of a long vacation for want of employment, — save only that then he brews work to broach in term-time. I find one so much delighted in law-sport, that when Lewis, the King of France, offered to ease him of a number of suits, he earnestly besought his Highness to leave him some twenty or thirty behind, wherewith he might merrily pass away the time.

He hath this property of an honest man that his word is as good as his bond; for he will pick the lock of the strongest conveyance, or creep out at the lattice of a word. Wherefore, he counts to enter common with others as good as his own several; for he will so vex his partners that they had rather forego their right than undergo a suit with him. As for the trumpeter barrator,

He falls in with all his neighbors that fall out, and spurs them on to go to law. A gentleman, who in a duel was rather scratched than wounded, sent for a chirurgeon, who, having opened the wound, charged his man with all speed to fetch such a salve from such a place in his study. "Why," said the gentleman, "is the hurt so dangerous?" "Oh yes," answered the chirurgeon, "if he returns not in post-haste, the wound will cure itself, and so I shall lose my fee." Thus the barrator posts to the houses of his neighbors, lest the sparks of their small discords should go out before he brings them fuel, and so he be broken by their making up. Surely, he loves not to have the bells rung in a peal, but he likes it rather when they are jangled backward, himself having kindled the fire of dissension amongst his neighbors.

He lives till his clothes have as many rents as himself hath made dissensions. I wonder any should be of this trade when none ever thrived on 't; paying dear rates for their counsels for bringing many cracked titles, they are fain to fill up their gaping chinks with the more gold.

But I have done with this wrangling companion, half afraid to meddle with him any longer, lest he should commence a suit against me for describing him.

The reader may easily perceive how this book of the Profane State would swell to a great proportion, should we therein character all the kinds of vicious persons which stand in opposition to those which are good. But this pains may well be spared, seeing that *rectum est index sui et obliqui;* and the lustre of the good formerly described will sufficiently discover the enormity of those which are otherwise.

THE DEGENEROUS GENTLEMAN.

SOME will challenge this title of incongruity, as if those two words were so dissonant that a whole sentence cannot hold them; for, sure, where the gentleman is the root, degenerous cannot be the fruit. But if any quarrel with my words, Valerius Maximus shall be my champion, who styleth such *nobilia portenta.* By gentleman we understand one whom the heralds (except they will deny their best records) must allow of ancient parentage. Such a one, when a child, being kept the devil's Nazarite, that no razor of correction must come upon his head in his father's family, see what he proves in the process of time, brought to extreme poverty. Herein we intend no invective glance on those pious gentlemen whose states are consumed through God's secret judgment, and none of the owners' visible default;

only we meddle with such as by carelessness and riot cause their own ruin.

He goes to school to learn in jest, and play in earnest. Now this gentleman, now that gentlewoman, begs him a play-day; and now the book must be thrown away that he may see the buck hunted. He comes to school late, departs soon, and the whole year with him, like the fortnight when Christmas-day falls on a Tuesday, is all holidays and half-holidays. And as the poets feign of Thetis, that she drenched Achilles her son in the Stygian waters that he might not be wounded with any weapon, so cockering mothers enchant their sons to make them rod-free, which they do by making some golden circles in the hand of the schoolmaster. Thus these two conjoining together, make the indentures to bind the youth to eternal ignorance. Yet perchance he may get some alms of learning; here a snap, there a piece of knowledge, but nothing to purpose.

His father's serving-men (which he counts no mean preferment) admit him into their society. Going to a drinking-match, they carry him with them to enter him, and applaud his hopefulness, finding him vicious beyond his age. The butler makes him free (having first paid his fees accustomed) of his own father's cellar, and guesseth the profoundness of his young master's capacity by the depth of the whole-ones he fetcheth off.

Coming to the university, his chief study is to study nothing. What is learning but a cloak-bag of books, cumbersome for a gentleman to carry? and the Muses fit to make wives for farmers' sons. Perchance his own tutor, for the promise of the next living, (which, notwithstanding his promise, he afterwards sells to another,) contributes to his undoing, letting him live as he list. Yea, perhaps his own mother, whilst his father diets him for his health with a moderate allowance, makes him surfeit underhand by sending him money. Thus whilst some complain that the university infected him, he infected the university, from which he sucked no milk, but poisoned her nipples.

At the inns of court, under pretence to learn law, he learns to be lawless; not knowing by his study so much as what an execution means, till he learns it by his own dear experience. Here he grows acquainted with the roaring boys, I am afraid so called by a woful prolepsis, here, for hereafter. What formerly was counted the chief credit of an orator, these esteem the honor of a swearer; pronunciation, to mouth an oath with a graceless grace. These, as David saith, "clothe themselves with curses as with a garment," and therefore desire to be in the latest fashion both in their clothes and curses.

These infuse all their skill into their young novice, who shortly proves such a proficient that he exceeds his masters in all kinds of vicious courses.

Through the mediation of a scrivener, he grows acquainted with some great usurer. Nor is this youngster so ravenous as the other is ready to feed him with money, sometimes with a courteous violence forcing on him more than he desires, provided the security be good; except the usurer be so valiant as to hazard the losing of a small hook to catch a great fish, and will adventure to trust him, if his estate in hope be over measure, though he himself be under age. Now the greater part of the money he takes up is not for his own spending, but to pay the shot of other men's riot.

After his father's death, he flies out more than ever before. Formerly he took care for means for his spending, now he takes care for spending for his means. His wealth is so deep a gulf, no riot can ever sound the bottom of it. To make his guests drunk is the only seal of their welcome. His very meanest servant may be master of the cellar, and those who deserve no beer may command the best wine: such dancing by day, such masking by night; such roaring, such revelling, able to awake the sleeping ashes of his great-great-grandfather, and to fright all blessing from his house.

Meantime the old sore of his debts corrupts and festers. He is careless to take out the dead flesh, or to discharge either principal or interest. Such small leaks are not worth the stopping or searching for till they be greater; he should undervalue himself to pay a sum before it grew considerable for a man of his estate. Nor can he be more careless to pay than the usurer is willing to continue the debt, knowing that his bonds, like infants, battil best with sleeping.

Vacation is his vocation, and he scorns to follow any profession, and will not be confined to any laudable employment. But they who count a calling a prison, shall at last make a prison their calling. He instils also his lazy principles into his children, being of the same opinion with the Neapolitan gentry, who stand so on the puntos of their honor that they prefer robbery before industry, and will rather suffer their daughter to make merchandise of her chastity than marry the richest merchant.

Drinking is one of the principal liberal sciences he professeth,—a most ungenteel quality, fit to be banished to rogues and rags. It was anciently counted a Dutch vice, and swarmed most in that country. I remember a sad accident which happened to Fliolmus, King of Gothland, who, whilst a lord of misrule ruled in his court, and both he and his servants were drunk, in mere merriment, meaning no harm, they took the king and put him in jest into a great vessel of beer, and drowned him in earnest. But one tells us that this ancient and habited vice is amongst the Dutch of late years much decreased; which if it be not, would it were. Sure our mariners observe, that, as the sea grows daily shallower and shallower on the shores of Holland and Zealand, so the channel of late waxeth deeper on the coasts of Kent and Essex. I pray God, if drunkenness ebbs in Dutchland, it doth not flow in England, and gain not in the island what it loseth in the continent. Yea, some plead when overwhelmed with liquor that their thirst is but quenched; as well may they say that in Noah's flood the dust was but sufficiently allayed.

Gaming is another art he studies much,—an enticing witch that hath caused the ruin of many. Hannibal said of Marcellus, that *nec bonam nec malam fortunam ferre potest*; he could be quiet neither conqueror nor conquered: thus such is the itch of play, that gamesters neither winning nor losing can rest contented. One propounded this question, whether men in ships on sea were to be accounted among the living or the dead, because there were but few inches betwixt them and drowning. The same scruple may be made of great gamesters, though their estates be never so great, whether they are to be esteemed poor or rich, there being but a few casts at dice betwixt a gentleman (in great game) and a beggar. Our gallant games deeply, and makes no doubt in conscience to adventure advowsons, patronages, and church-livings in gaming. He might call to mind Sir Miles Pateridge, who (as the soldiers cast lots for Christ his coat) played at dice for Jesus' bells with King Henry the Eighth, and won them of him. Thus he brought the bells to ring in his pocket, but the ropes afterwards catched about his neck, and for some offences he was hanged in the days of King Edward the Sixth.

Then first he sells the outworks of his state, some straggling manor. Nor is he sensible of this sale, which makes his means more entire, as counting the gathering of such scattering rents rather burdensome than profitable. This he sells at half the value, so that the feathers will buy the goose, and the wood will pay for the ground. With this money, if he stops the hole to one creditor, by his prodigality he presently opens a wider gap to another.

By this time the long dormant usurer ramps for the payment of his money. The principal, the grandmother, and the use, the daughter, and the use upon use, the grandchild, and perchance a generation farther, hath swelled the debt to an incredible sum, for the satisfying whereof our gallant sells the moiety of his estate.

Having sold half his land, he abates nothing of his expenses, but thinks five hundred pounds a year will be enough to maintain that for which a thousand pound was too little. He will not stoop till he falls, nor lessen his kennel of dogs till, with Actæon, he be eaten up with his own hounds.

Being about to sink, he catcheth at every rush to save himself. Perchance sometimes he snatcheth at the thistle of a project, which first pricks his hands and then breaks. Herein, it may be, he adventured on a matter wherein he had no skill himself, (hoping, by letting the commonwealth blood, to fill up his own veins again,) and therefore trades with his partner's brains, as his partner with his purse, till both miscarry together; or else it may be he catcheth hold on the heel of another man who is in as dangerous a case as himself, and they embracing each other in mutual bonds, hasten their drowning together. His last manor he sells twice, to a country gentleman and a London usurer, — though the last, as having the first title, prevails to possess it; usurers herein being like unto foxes; they seldom take pains to dig any holes themselves, but earth in that which the foolish badger made for them, and dwell in the manors and fair houses which others have built and provided.

Having lost his own legs, he relies on the staff of his kindred; first visiting them as an intermitting ague, but afterwards turns a quotidian, wearing their thresholds as bare as his own coat. At last, he is as welcome as a storm; he that is abroad shelters himself from it, and he that is at home shuts the door. If he intrudes himself yet, some with their jeering tongues give him many a gird, but his brazen impudence feels nothing; and let him be armed on free-cost with the pot and the pipe, he will give them leave to shoot their flouts at him till they be weary. Sometimes he sadly paceth over the ground he sold, and is on fire with anger with himself for his folly, but presently quencheth it at the next alehouse.

Having undone himself, he sets up the trade to undo others. If he can but screw himself into the acquaintance of a rich heir, he rejoiceth as much at the prize as the Hollanders when they had intercepted the Plate fleet. He tutors this young gamester in vice, leading him a more compendious way to his ruin than possibly he could find out of himself. And doth not the guide deserve good wages for his direction?

Perhaps he behaves himself so basely that he is degraded, — the sad and solemn ceremonies whereof we may meet with in old precedents;

but of them all, in my apprehension, none should make deeper impression in an ingenuous soul than this one, that at the solemn degradation of a knight for high misdemeanor, the king and twelve knights more did put on mourning garments as an emblem of sorrow for this injury to honor, that a man, gentle by birth and blood, or honored by a prince's favor, should so far forget not only himself but his order as to deserve so severe punishment.

His death is as miserable as his life hath been vicious. An hospital is the height he hopes to be advanced to; but commonly he dies not in so charitable a prison, but sings his last note in a cage. Nor is it impossible but that, wanting land of his own, he may encroach on the king's highway; and there, taking himself to be lord of the soil, seize on travellers as strays due unto him, and so the hangman give him a wreath more than he had in his arms before. If he dies at liberty, in his pilgrimage betwixt the houses of his acquaintance, perhaps some well-disposed gentleman may pay for his burial, and truly mourn at the funeral of an ancient family. His children, if any, must seek their fortunes the farther off, because their father found his too soon, before he had wisdom to manage them. Within two generations his name is quite forgotten, that ever any such was in the place, except some herald in his visitation pass by, and chance to spell his broken arms in a church-window. And then how weak a thing is gentry, than which (if it wants virtue) brittle glass is the more lasting monument!

THE TRAITOR.

A TRAITOR works by fraud, as a rebel does by force, and in this respect is more dangerous, because there 's less stock required to set him up. Rebellion must be managed with many swords; treason to his prince's person may be with one knife. Generally their success is as bad as their cause, being either detected before, defeated in, or punished after their part acted; detected before, either by wilfulness or weakness of those which are privy to it.

A plotter of treason puts his head into the halter, and the halter into his hand to whom he first imparts it. He oftentimes reveals it, and by making a footstool of his friend's head, climbs up the higher into the prince's favor.

Some men's souls are not strong enough but that a weighty secret will work a hole through them. These, rather out of folly than falseness, unawares let fall words which are taken up by the judicious ears of such who can spell treason by putting together distracted syllables and by piecing of broken sentences. Others have their hearts swollen so great with hope of what they shall get that their bodies are too little to hold them, and so betray themselves by threatenings and blustering language. Others have cut their throats with their own hands, — their own writings, the best records, being produced against them. And here we must know, that

Strong presumptions sometimes serve for proofs in point of treason; for it being a deed of darkness, it is madness to look that the sun should shine at midnight, and to expect evident proof. Should princes delay till they did plainly see treason, they might chance to feel it first. If this *semiplena probatio* lights on a party suspected before, the party himself is the other part of the proof, and makes it complete. And here the rack, though fame-like it be

"Tam ficti pravique tenax, quam nuncia veri,"

is often used; and the wooden horse hath told strange secrets. But grant it pass undiscovered in the plotting, it is commonly prevented in the practising,

By the majesty, innocency, or valor of the prince or his attendants. Some have been dazzled with the divine beams shining in a prince's face, so that coming to command his life, they could not be masters of their own senses. Innocency hath protected others, and made their enemies relent; and pity, though a stranger to him for many years before, hath visited a traitor's heart in that very instant. If these fail, a king's valor hath defended him; it being most true of a king what Pliny reports of a lion, in hunting if he be wounded and not killed, he will be sure to eye and kill him that wounded him.

Some, by flourishing aforehand, have never stricken a blow; but by warning have armed those to whom they threatened. Thus mad Somerville, coming to kill Queen Elizabeth, by the way (belike to try whether his sword would cut) quarrelled with and wounded one or two, and therefore was apprehended before he came to the court.

The palsy of guiltiness hath made the stoutest traitors' hands to shake, sometimes to miss their mark. Their conscience, sleeping before, is then awakened with this crying sin. The way seems but short to a traveller when he views it from the top of a hill, who finds it very long when he comes into the plain: so treason, surveyed in the heat of blood and from the height of passion, seems easy to be effected; which, reviewed in cold blood, on even terms, is full of dangers and difficulties. If it speed in the acting, generally it 's revenged afterwards: for,

A king though killed is not killed, so long as he hath son or subject surviving. Many who have thought they have discharged the debt, have been broken afterwards with the arrearages. As for journeymen-traitors, who work for others, their wages are ever paid them with a halter; and where one gaineth a garland of bays, hundreds have had a wreath of hemp.

THE TYRANT.

A TYRANT is one whose list is his law, making his subjects his slaves. Yet that is but a tottering kingdom which is founded on trembling people, which fear and hate their sovereign.

He gets all places of advantage into his own hands; yea, he would disarm his subjects of all scythes and pruning-hooks, but for fear of a general rebellion of weeds and thistles in the land.

He takes the laws at the first rather by undermining than assault; and therefore, to do unjustly with the more justice, he counterfeits a legality in all his proceedings, and will not butcher a man without a statute for it.

Afterwards he rageth freely in innocent blood. Is any man virtuous? then he is a traitor, and let him die for it who durst presume to be good when his prince is bad. Is he beloved? he is a rebel, hath proclaimed himself king, and reigns already in people's affections; it must cost him his life. Is he of kin to the crown, though so far off that his alliance is scarce to be derived? all the veins of his body must be drained and emptied, to find there and fetch thence that dangerous drop of royal blood. And thus having taken the prime men away, the rest are easily subdued. In all these particulars Machiavel is his only counsellor; who, in his "Prince," seems to him to resolve all these cases of conscience to be very lawful.

Worst men are his greatest favorites. He keeps a constant kennel of bloodhounds to accuse whom he pleaseth. These will depose more than any can suppose, not sticking to swear that they heard fishes speak, and saw through a millstone at midnight. These fear not to forswear, but fear they shall not forswear enough to cleave the pin and do the deed. The less credit they have the more they are believed, and their very accusation is held a proof.

He leaves nothing that his poor subjects can call their own but their miseries. And as in the West Indies thousands of kine are killed for their tallow alone, and their flesh cast away, so many men are murdered merely for their wealth, that other men may make mummy of the fat of their estates.

He counts men in misery the most melodious instruments: especially if they be well tuned and played upon by cunning musicians, who are artificial in tormenting them, the more the merrier; and if he hath a set and full concert of such tortured, miserable souls, he danceth most cheerfully at the pleasant ditty of their dying groans. He loves not to be prodigal of men's lives, but thriftily improves the objects of his cruelty, spending them by degrees, and epicurizing on their pain; so that, as Philoxenus wished a crane's throat, he could desire asses' ears, the longer to entertain their hideous and miserable roaring. Thus nature had not racks enough for men (the colic, gout, stone, &c.) but art must add to them, and devils in flesh antedate hell here in inventing torments: which, when inflicted on malefactors, extort pity from merciful beholders, (and make them give what is not due,) but when used by tyrants on innocent people, such tender hearts as stand by suffer what they see, and by the proxy of sympathy feel what they behold.

He seeks to suppress all memorials and writings of his actions; and as wicked Tereus, after he had ravished Philomela, cut out her tongue, so, when tyrants have wronged and abused the times they live in, they endeavor to make them speechless to tell no tales to posterity. Herein their folly is more to be admired than their malice, for learning can never be drained dry. Though it may be dammed up for one age, yet it will break over; and historians' pens, being long kept fasting, will afterwards feed more greedily on the memories of tyrants, and describe them to the full. Yea, I believe their ink hath made some tyrants blacker than they were in their true complexion.

At last he is haunted with the terrors of his own conscience. If any two do but whisper together (whatsoever the propositions be), he conceives their discourse concludes against him. Company and solitariness are equally dreadful unto him, being never safe; and he wants a guard to guard him from his guard, and so proceeds *in infinitum.* The scouts of Charles, Duke of Burgundy, brought him news that the French army was hard by, being nothing else but a field full of high thistles, whose tops they mistook for so many spears. On lesser ground this tyrant conceives greater fears. Thus in vain doth he seek to fence himself from without, whose foe is within him.

He is glad to patch up a bad night's sleep out of pieces of slumber. They seldom sleep soundly who have blood for their bolster. His fancy presents him with strange masques, wherein only fiends and furies are actors. The fright awakes him, and he is no sooner glad that it was a dream but fears it is prophetical.

In vain he courts the friendship of foreign princes. They defy his amity, and will not join their clean hands with his bloody ones. Sometimes, to ingratiate himself, he doth some good acts; but virtue becomes him worse than vice, for all know he counterfeits it for his own ends.

Having lived in other men's blood, he dies commonly in his own. He had his will all his life, but seldom makes his testament at his death, being suddenly taken away, either by private hand or public insurrection. It is observed of the camel, that it lies quietly down till it hath its full load, and then riseth up. But this *vulgus* is a kind of beast which riseth up soonest when it is overladen; immoderate cruelty causing it to rebel. "*Fero*" is a fitter motto than "*Ferio*" for Christians in their carriage towards lawful authority, though unlawfully used.

THE END.

www.ingramcontent.com/pod-product-compliance
Lightning Source LLC
LaVergne TN
LVHW020216110826
845151LV00003B/735